Lip Flexibilities

for all brass instruments

Bai Lin

Central Conservatory of Music
Beijing, China

Exclusively Distributed by
Carl Fischer Music
48 Wall St., 28th floor
New York 10005

Balquhidder Music

Lip Flexibilities
for all brass instruments
Bai Lin *Central Conservatory of Music, Beijing, China*

Exclusively Distributed by
Carl Fischer Music
48 Wall St., 28th floor
New York NY 10005

BQ-38
ISBN 0-9630856-6-2
UPC 798408035471
Printed in the United States of America

© Copyright 1996 Bai Lin. Copyright assigned to Balquhidder Music, 1996, 2010, 2018
All Rights Reserved.

Published by *Balquhidder Music*
PO Box 856 Montrose CA 91021 USA   www.balquhiddermusic.com

BAI LIN

Bai Lin was born in Qiqihaer, China, in 1935. After studying music at Northeast LuXun Art and Music College from 1951 through 1954 he went to Hungary in 1955 for futher study at the Franz Liszt Academy of Music. There he studied trumpet with Jmre Lubik and composition with Andre Szervanszky, graduating in 1962.

He returned to China to teach at the Central Conservatory of Music in Beijing and soon became Chairman of the Wind and Percussion Department. He has played with the Chinese Modern Peking Opera Orchestra and has published "Selected Trumpet Solos" in China and has also composed pieces for brass ensemble.

He has many students from all parts of China and has been involved in trumpet pedagogy in many areas of the world including acting as a judge in 1984 in the 22nd International Budapest Trumpet Competition. He has often been a professor and judge at the Barcs International Brass Chamber Music Camp (Hungary) and made exchange visits to the Debrecen Conservatory of Music in Hungary as well as the Tokyo Arts University. He is now Trumpet Professor and Chairman of the Wind and Strings Department of the Central Conservatory of

　　柏林1935年生于中國齊齊哈爾市。1950年就讀東北魯迅藝術學院音樂系。1955年赴匈牙利留學,在布達佩斯李斯特音樂學院師從小號教授伊姆雷·魯比克先生,並同時與安德烈·雷爾萬斯基先生學習作曲。1962年以優異的成績畢業于該院。同年回國就職于北京中央音樂學院教授小號專業及銅管重奏,合奏和歐洲管樂藝術史等課。曾任管樂、打擊樂教研室主任兼任中國京劇院小號演奏員。編寫出版了"小號教學曲集"及中央音樂學院小號考級教程並創作改編了小號獨奏,銅管重奏曲多首。

　　1984年受聘為第二十二屆布達佩斯國際小號比賽評委。其後多次應邀為匈牙利"勃爾其"國際銅管研究班的教授及演奏比賽的評委。1990年赴匈牙利迪柏瑞森音樂學院講學;1994年在日本東京藝術大學講學和訪問。

　　柏林先生為中國的一些交響樂團及音樂院校培養了許多優秀的小號演奏家和教師,以及國際比賽獲獎者。他現任中央音樂學院管弦系主任,小號教授。

前 言

　　這套練習是北京中央音樂學院小號教學中關於嘴唇靈敏、柔軟訓練的教材之一。我希望本教材的練習內容能有助于學生們發展嘴唇的靈敏、輕巧、富有彈性，從而提高學生們的吹奏能力。

　　在編寫這套教材時，我力圖囊括那些我認為對這方面技巧訓練有重要價值的材料，按照教學規律，由淺入深，循序漸進，使本教材內容前後密切相接，具有序列性。

　　這套練習不論對初學者還是對具有較高吹奏能力的演奏者都很有實用價值，在我自己的練習過程中深感受益匪淺，通過教學實踐也證明對學生們也都是很有幫助的。

　　吹奏者依據自己嘴唇的不同狀況和演奏的需要可選擇本教材中的部分練習做為每日基本練習內容之一，有計劃的堅持練習。吹奏時嘴唇要鬆弛、自然，喉嚨、舌根，切勿緊張、氣流要通暢、飽滿、均勻穩定，努力去尋求你想像中的美好音質。然而當你嘴唇乏力或疲勞不適的時候，就應當選擇一些簡單的練習吹奏，而不要吹奏那些力所不及的高音練習，以免嘴唇受傷，或養成不良奏法。如果你按照正確的吹奏方法，根據自己的程度持久地循序漸進地吹奏一些本教材中適合你自己狀況的練習做為每日基本練習內容之一。我相信對你的吹奏是會產生良好的積極作用的，正像我已然體會到的一樣。

柏 林

1995年12月

Preface

This book was written for the trumpet students of the Central Conservatory of Music in Beijing, China. I hope the contents of this book can help students in developing their lip flexibility and their ability to play the trumpet.

I have tried hard to include all aspects of slurring technique and to trace the progression from the beginner to the advanced level. Therefore, the contents of this book are very helpful for the elementary was well as the advanced players. From my own practice and teaching experience I have seen this as useful to all my students.

During practice sessions your embouchure, throat and tongue should be naturally relaxed and flexible. The air should be fluid and steady (consistent). Always try to produce your most beautiful tone.

If you feel your embouchure is tiring or is uncomfortable, you should choose an easier section to practice. Do not attempt to play in too high a register. This will avoid hurting your embouchure or learning to play incorrectly.

The best way to practice these exercises is to concentrate only on the appropriate sections according to your level of development. Players according to their different embouchure condition and requirements can choose appropriate portions of this book to make their own daily practice.

I believe these exercises can create a positive influence in your playing. I have experienced such benefit from them in my own playing for many years.

Professor Bai Lin, Professor of Trumpet, Central Conservatory of Music,
Beijing, China 1996

Lip Flexibilities
for all brass instruments

Bai Lin

I.

2

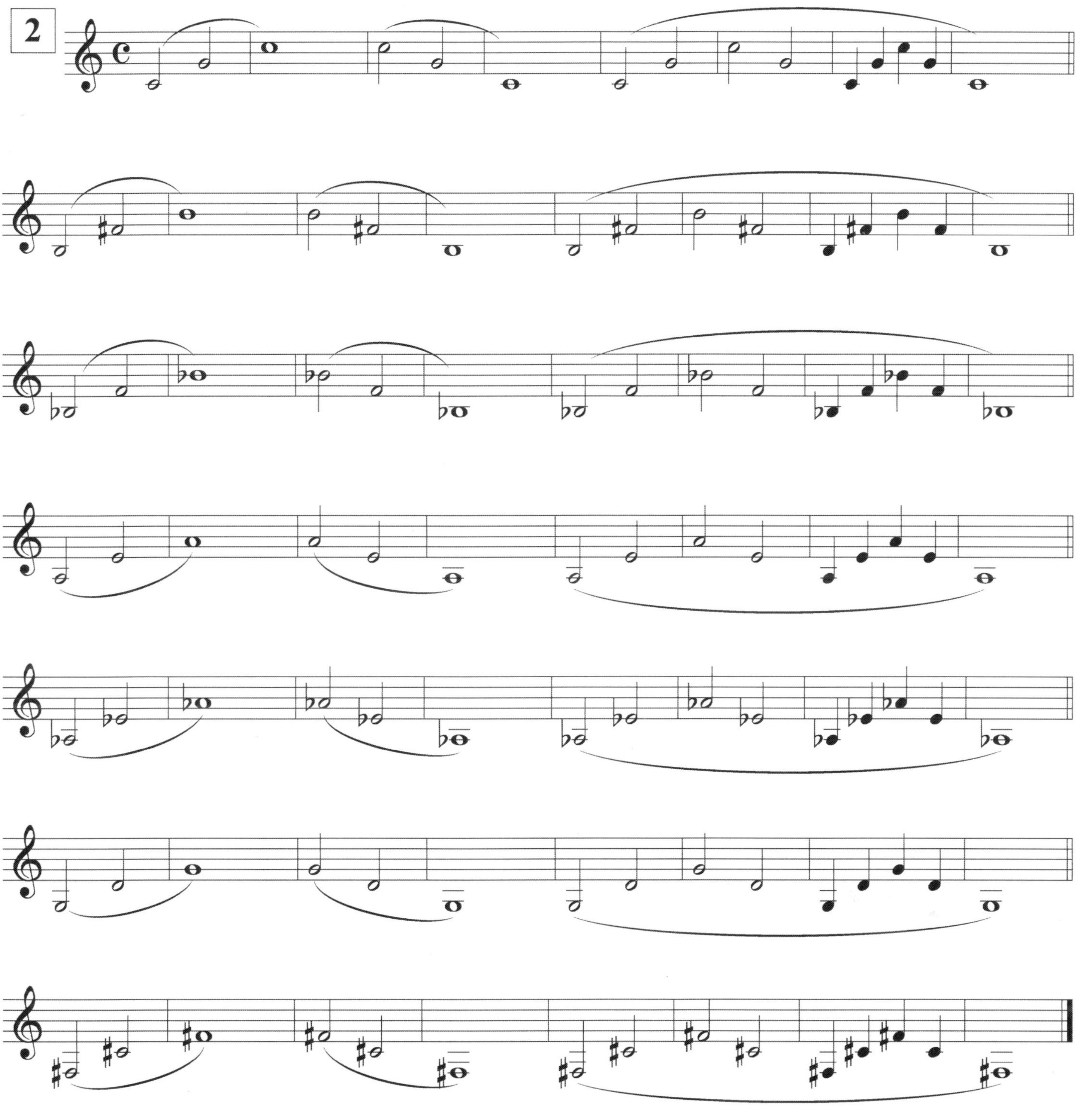

3

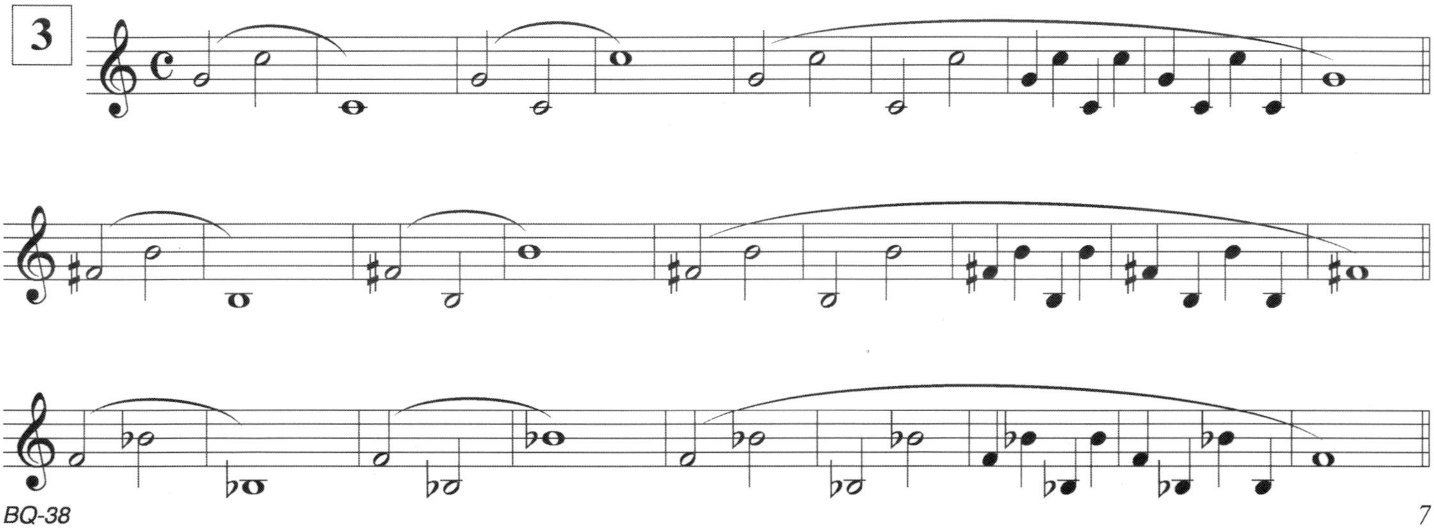

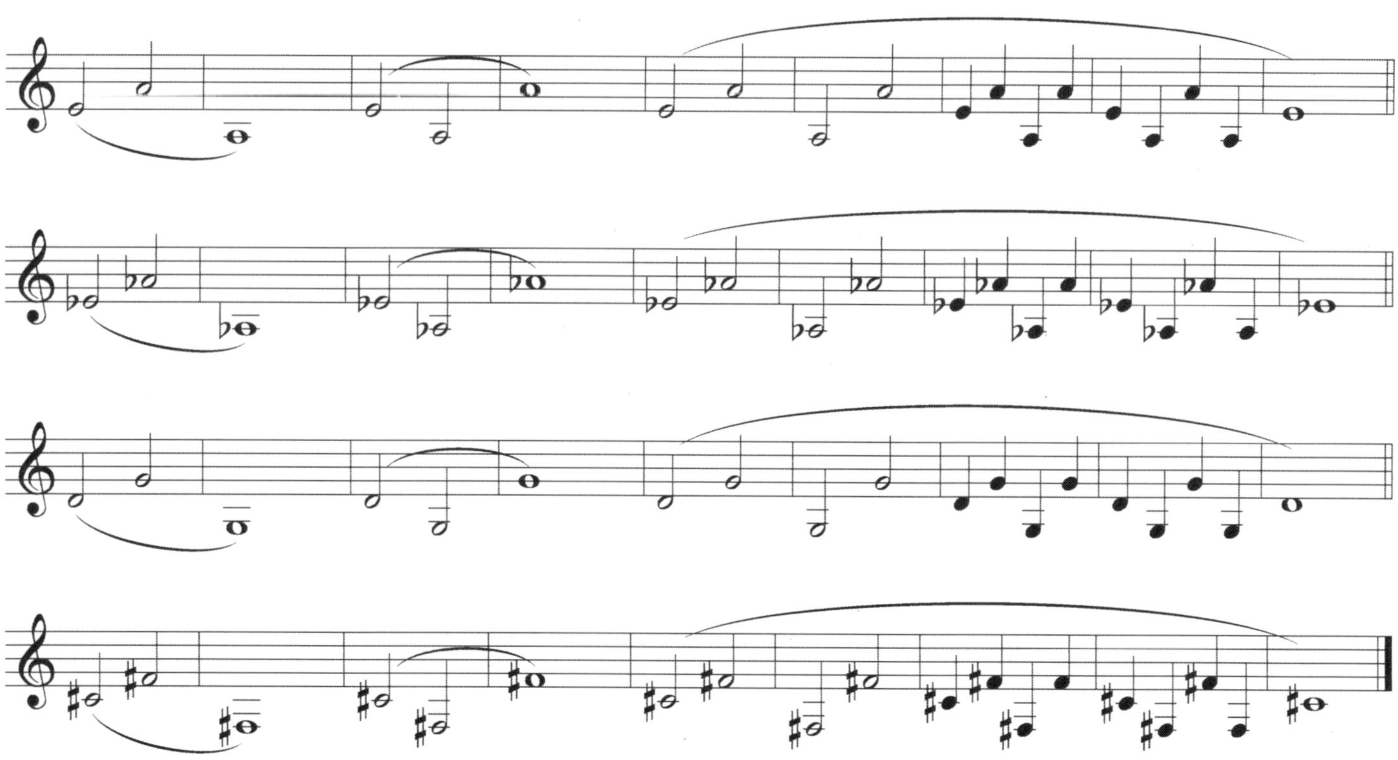

4

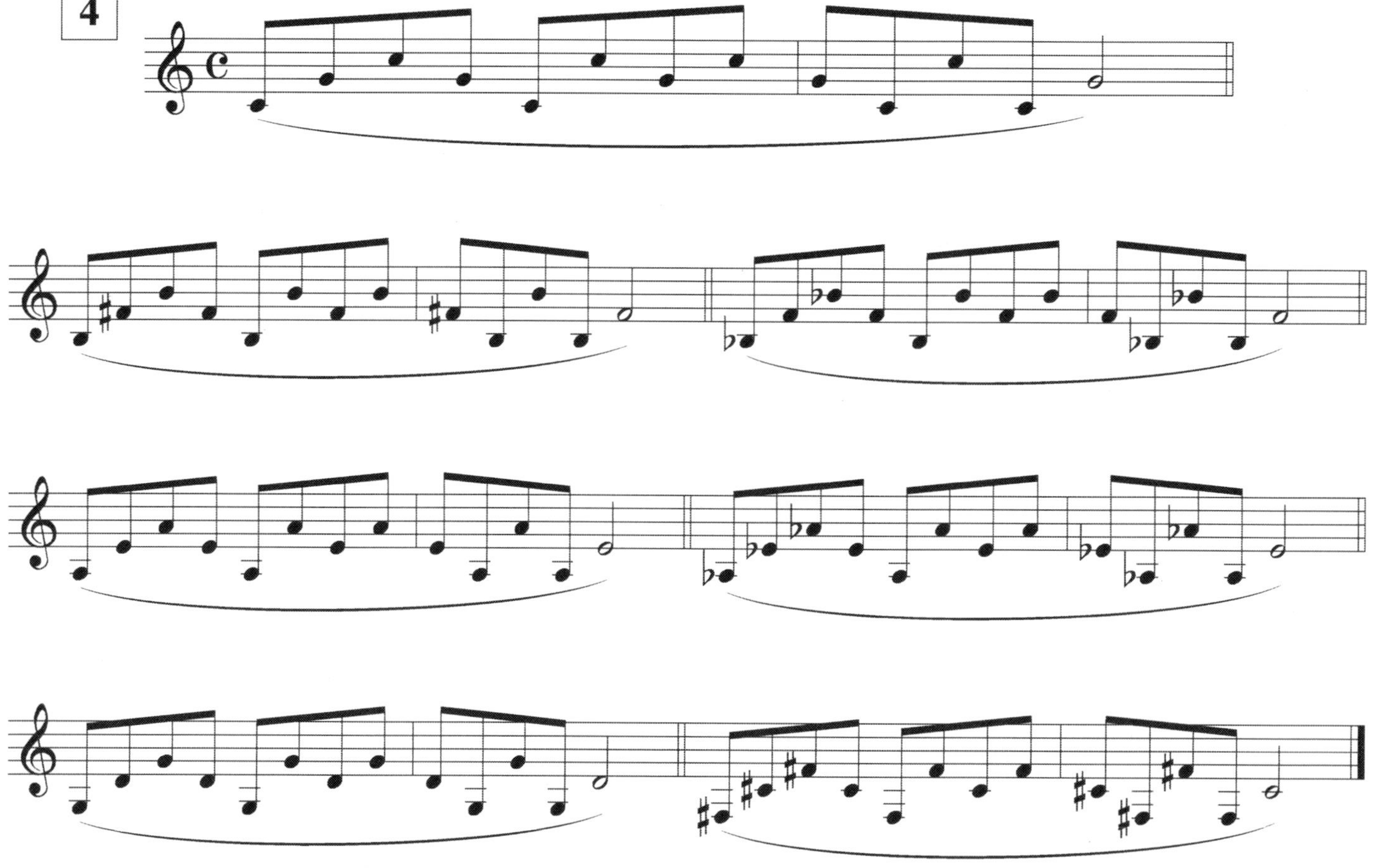

II.

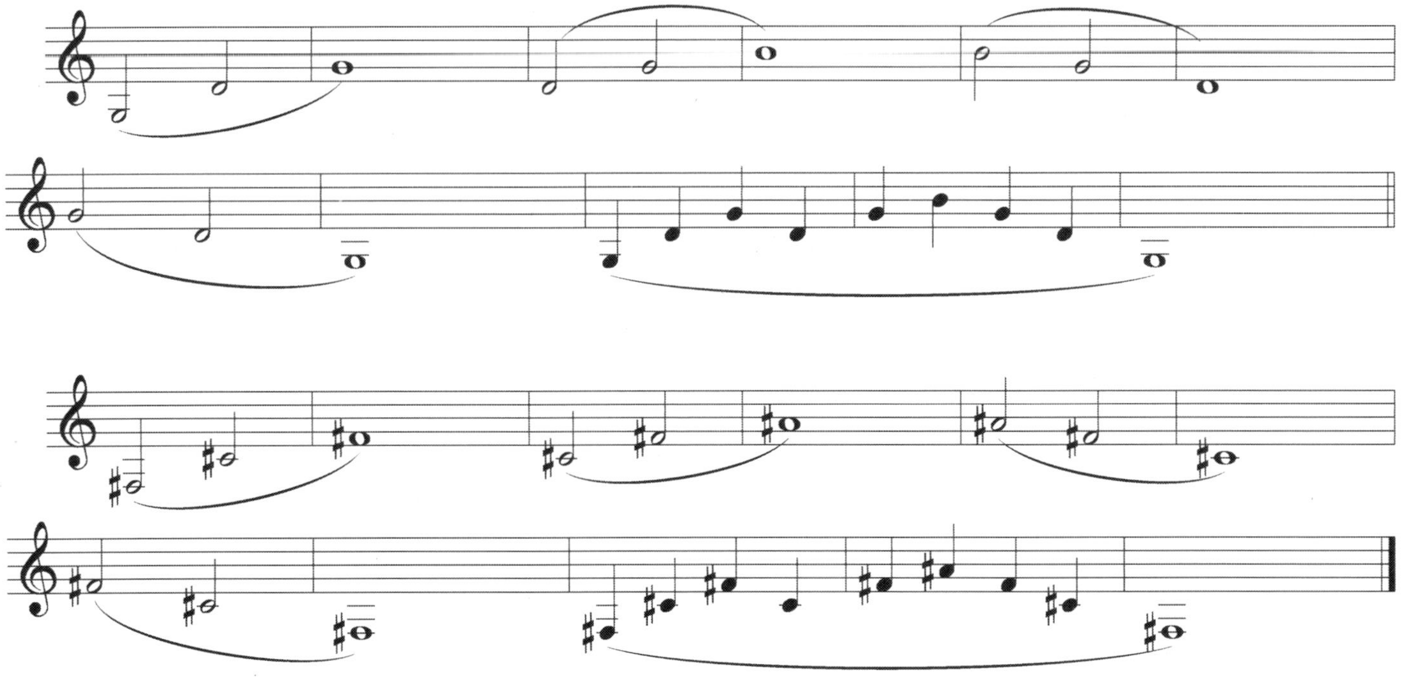

6

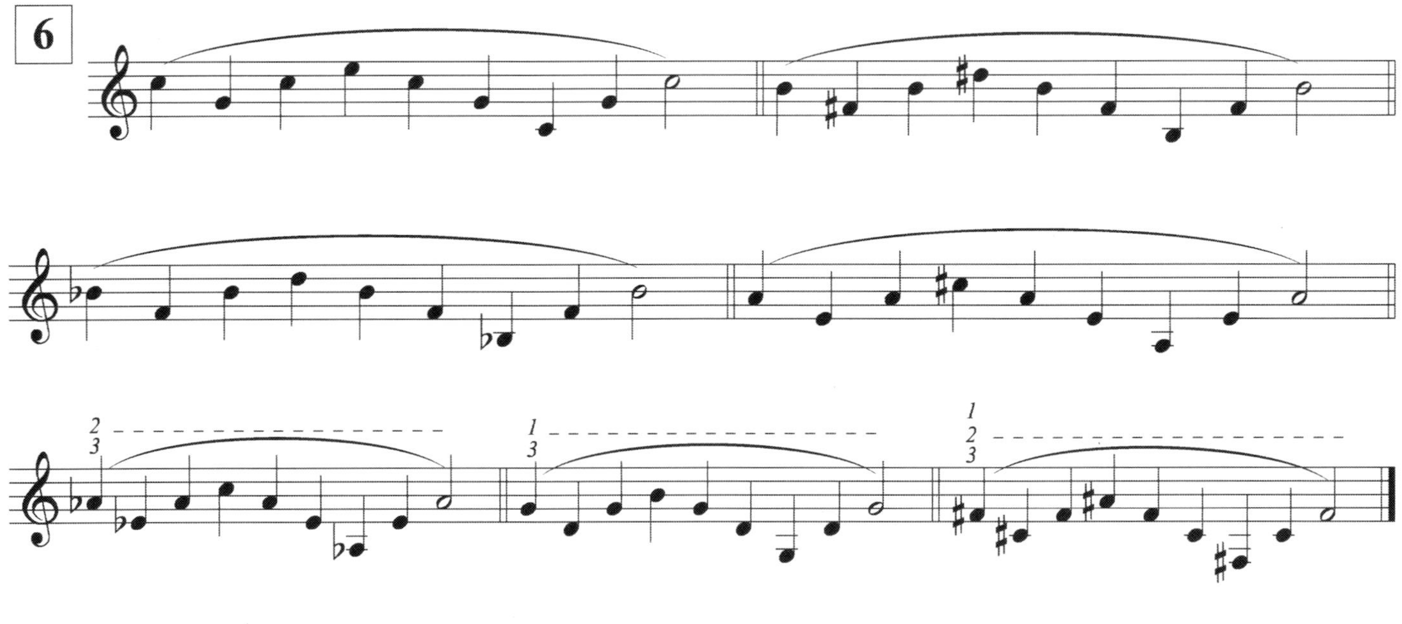

7

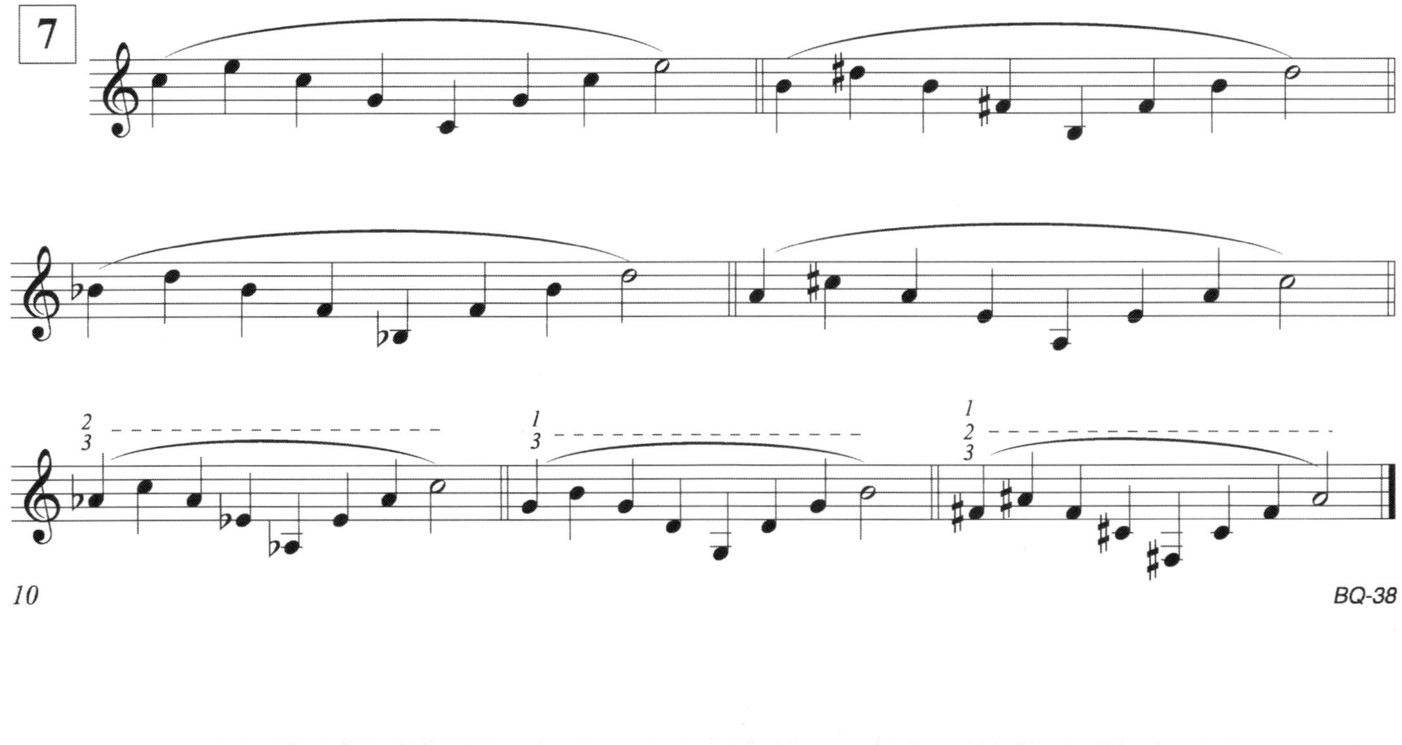

8

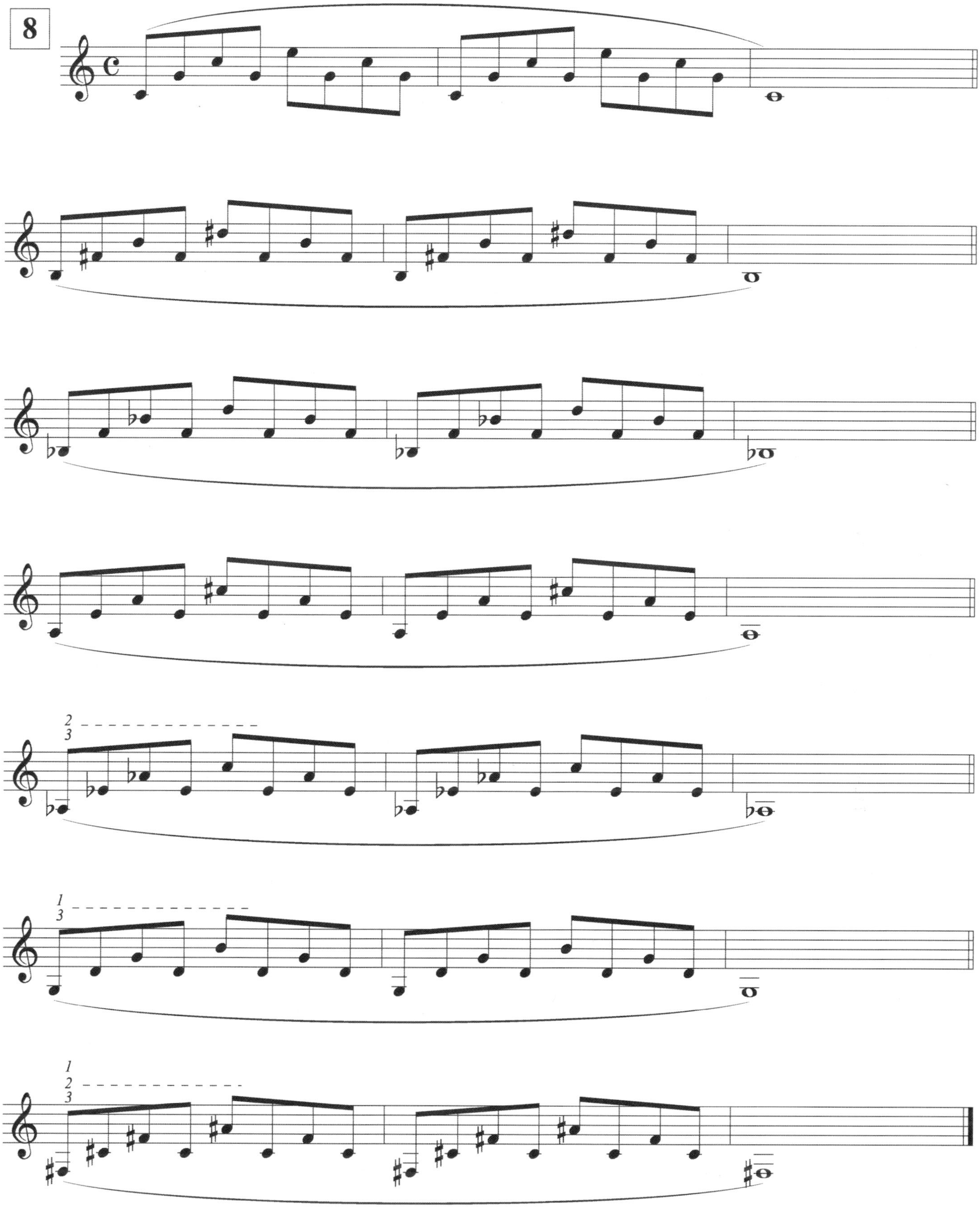

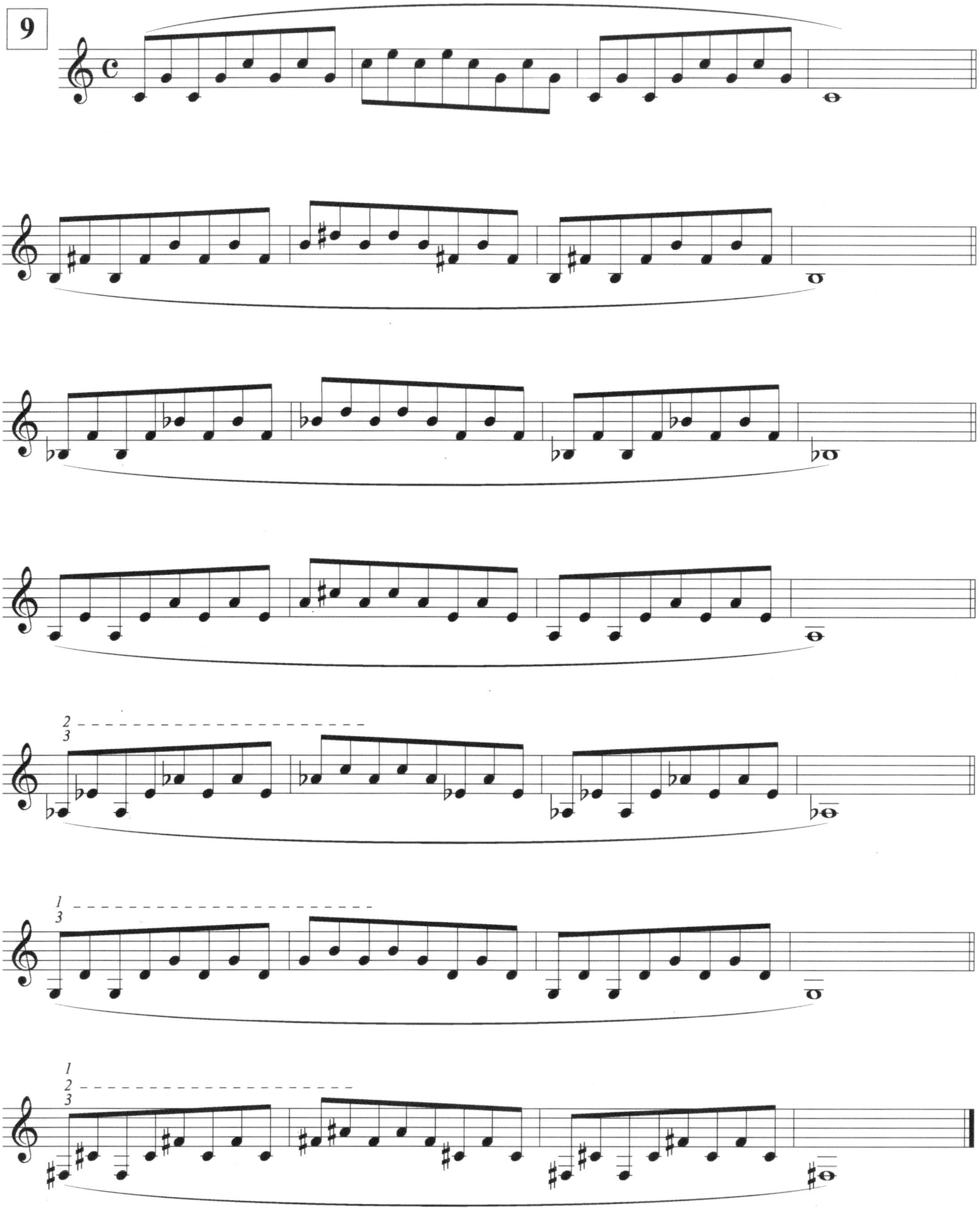
9
2
3
1
3
1
2
3

10

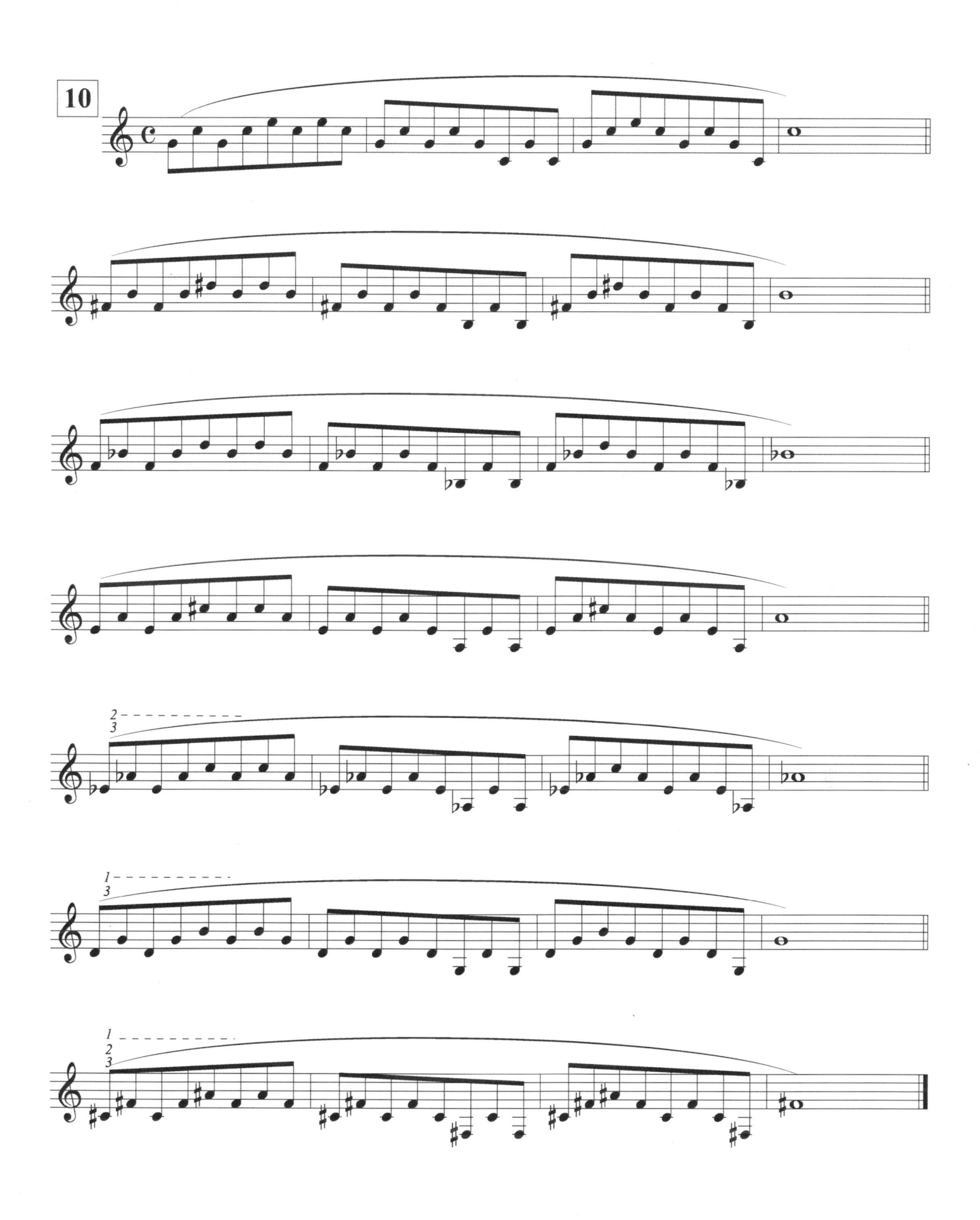

III.

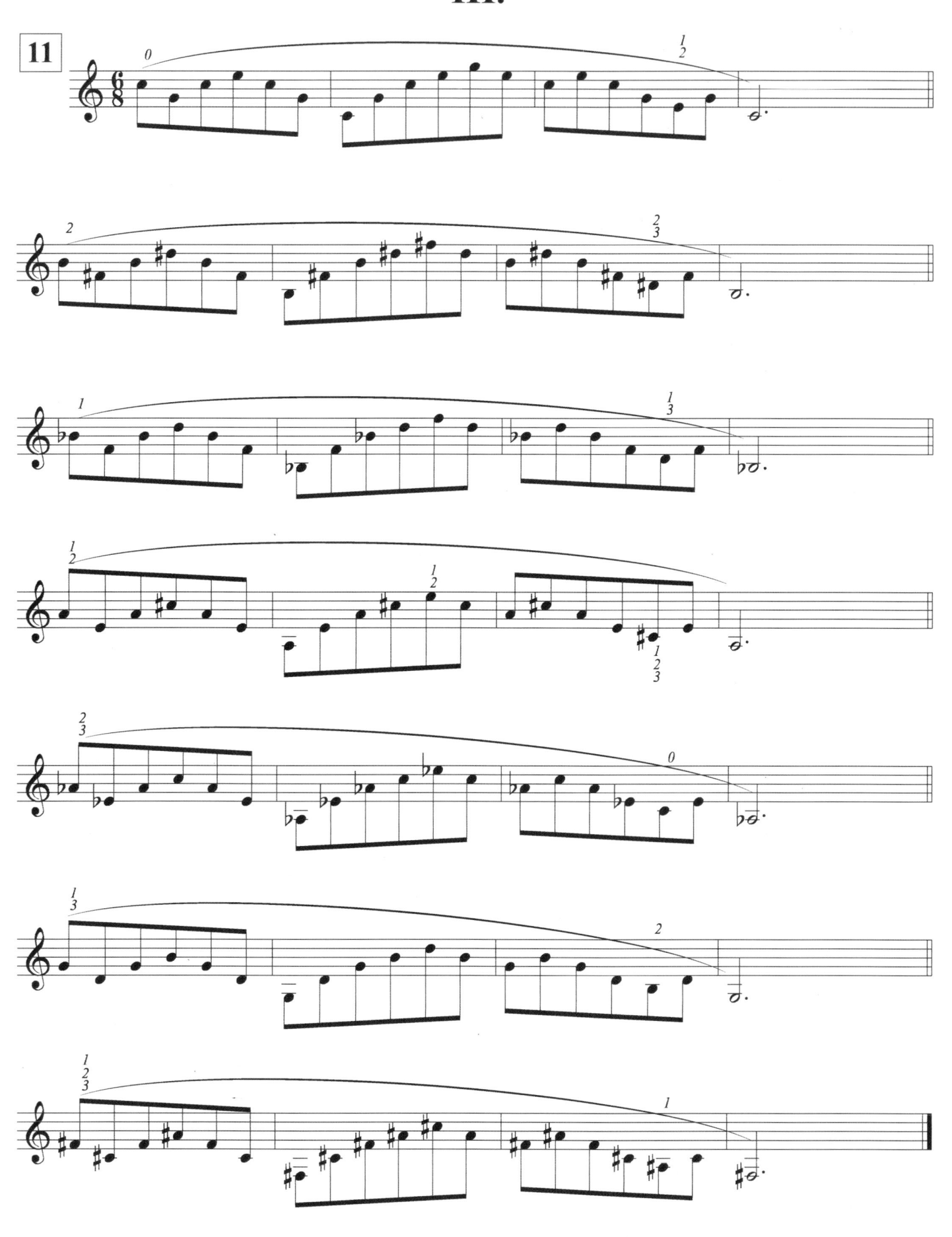

12

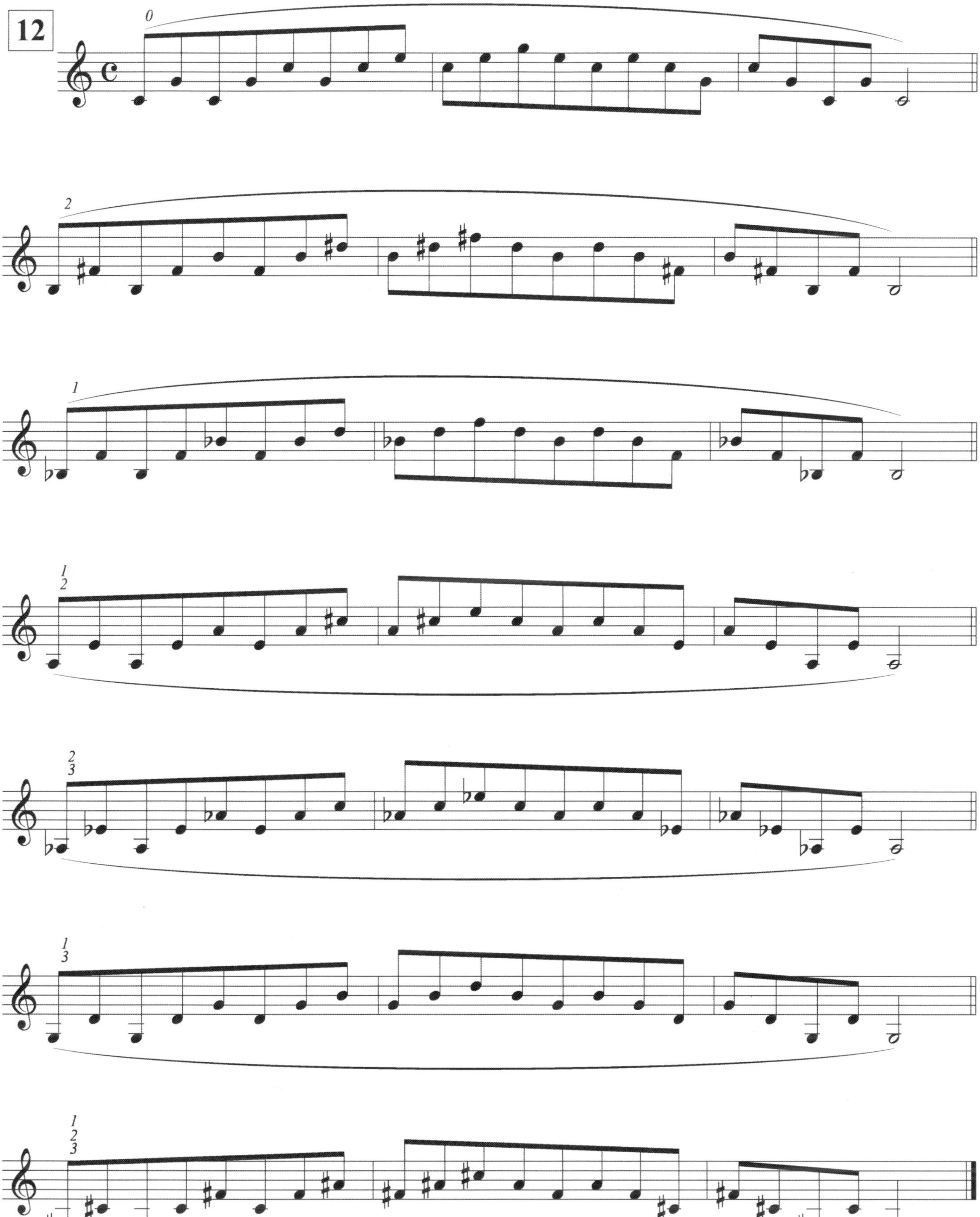

13

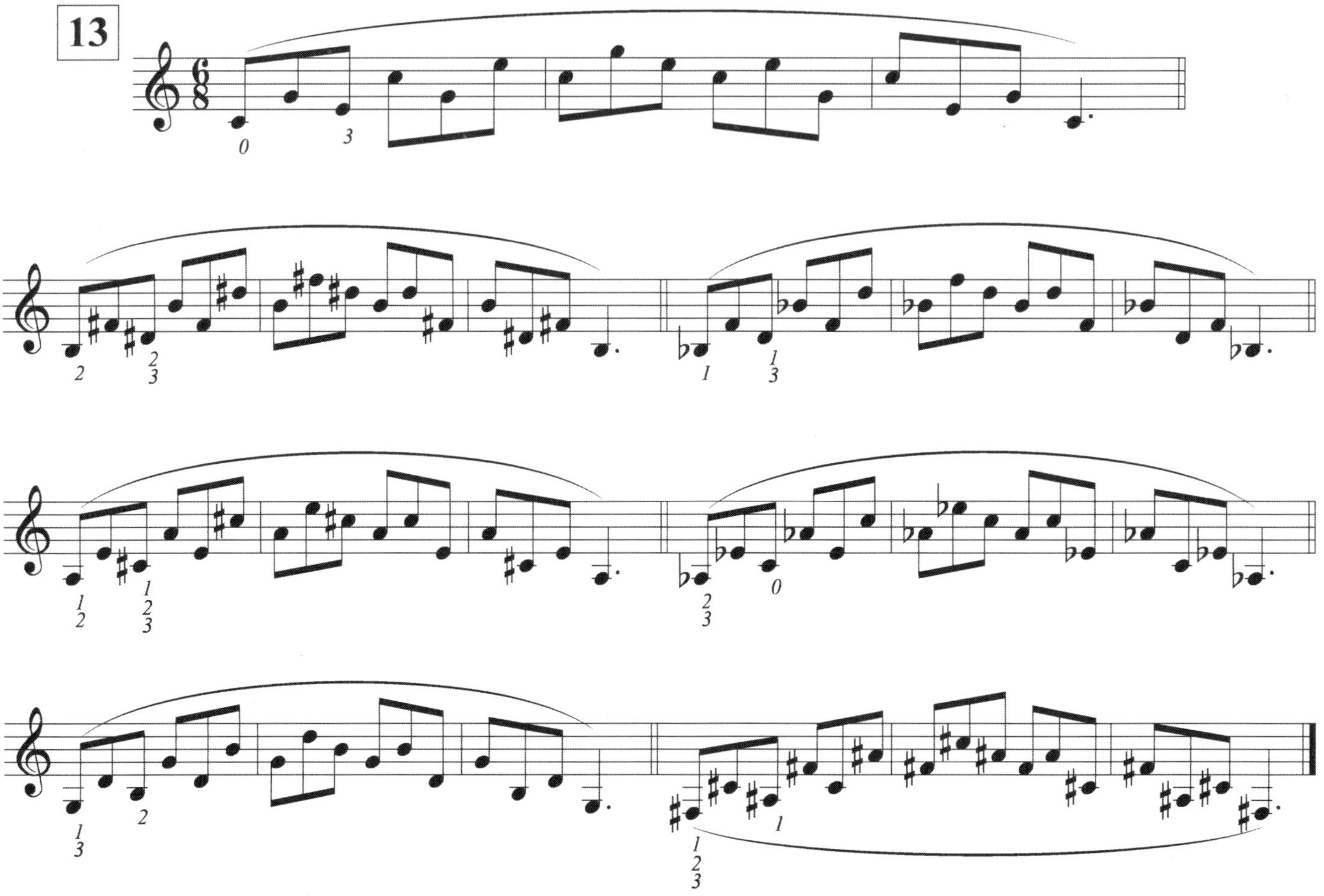

14

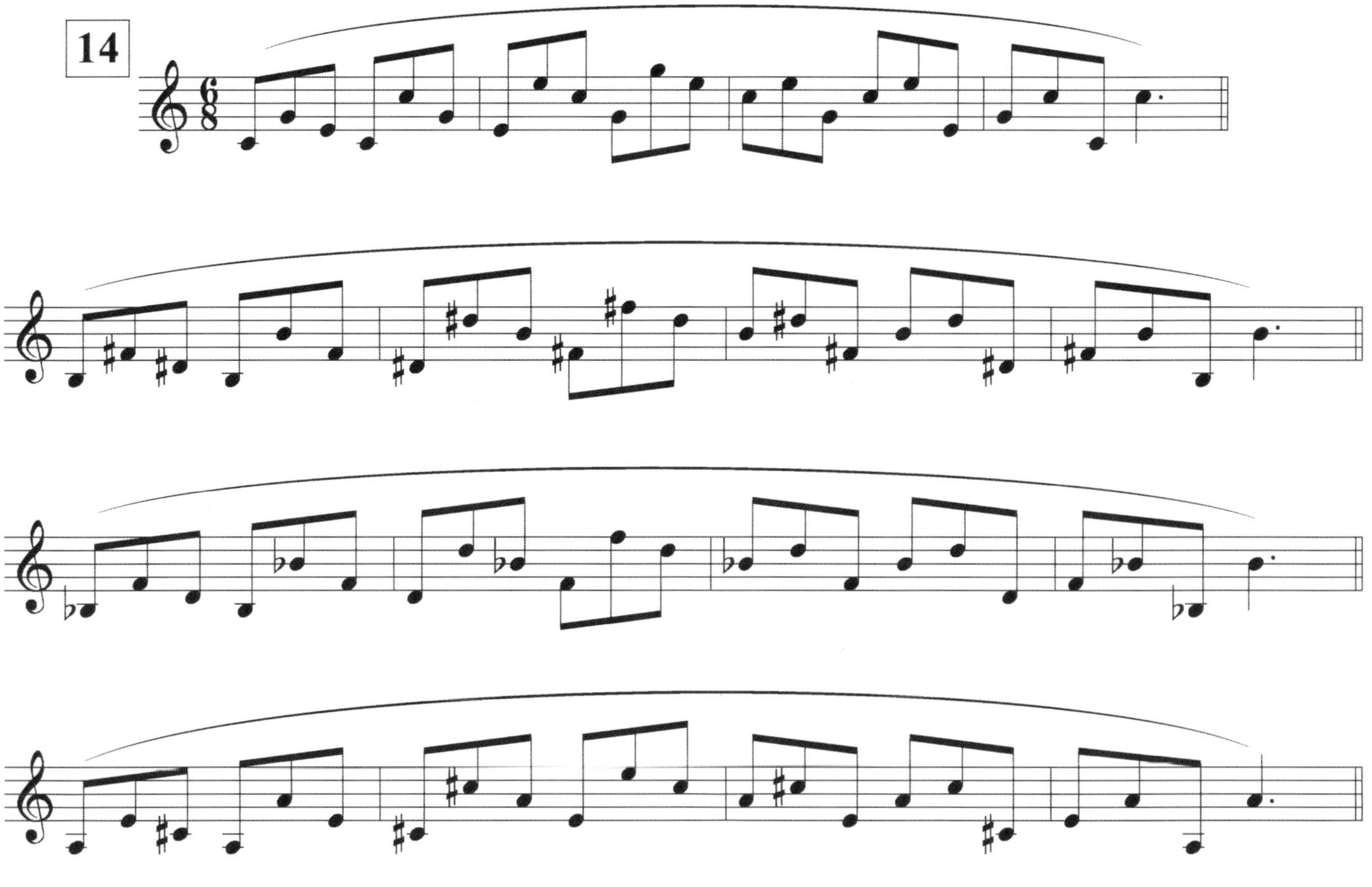

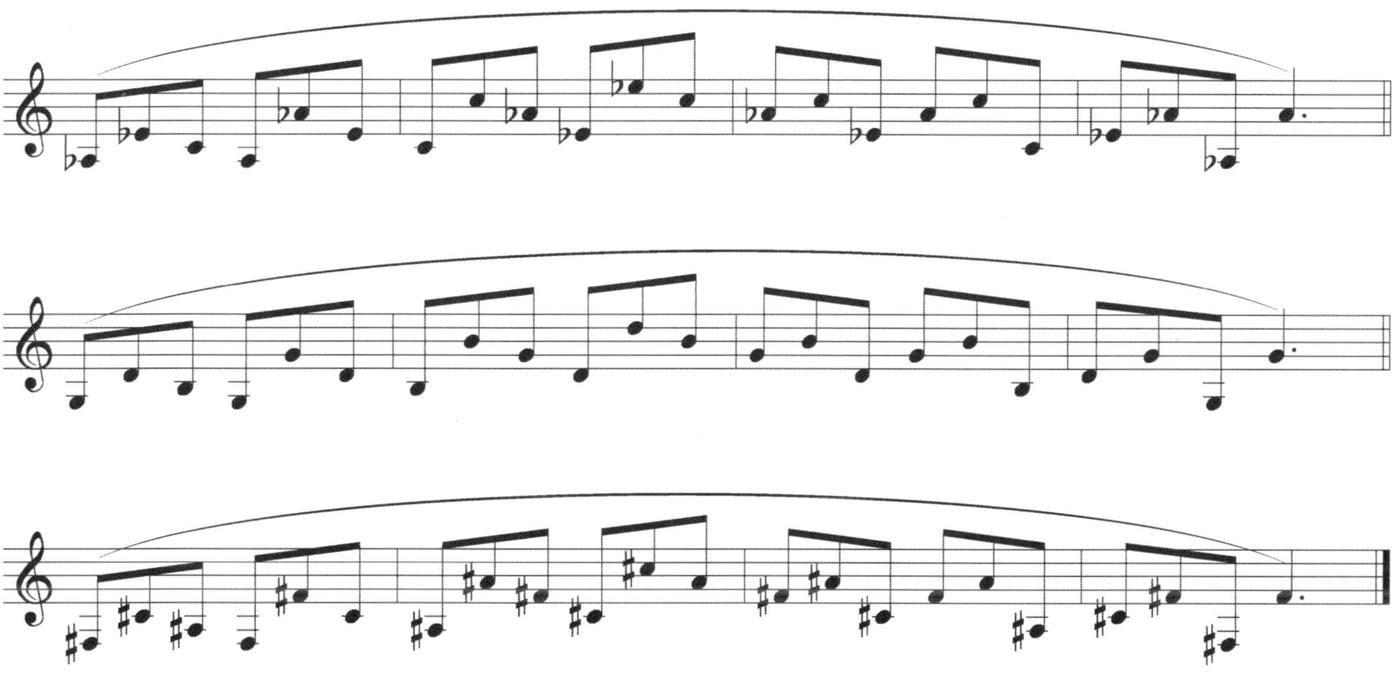

15

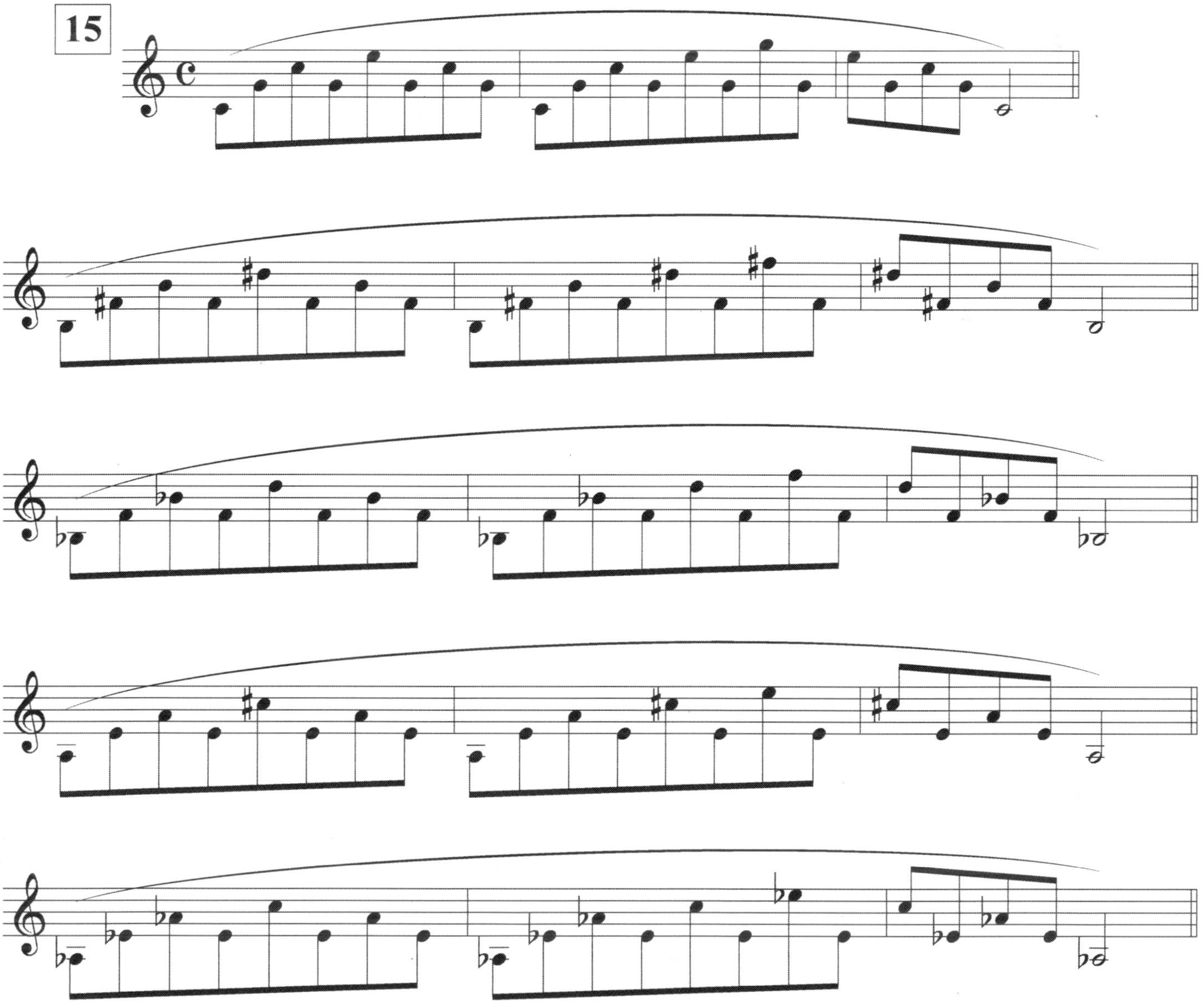

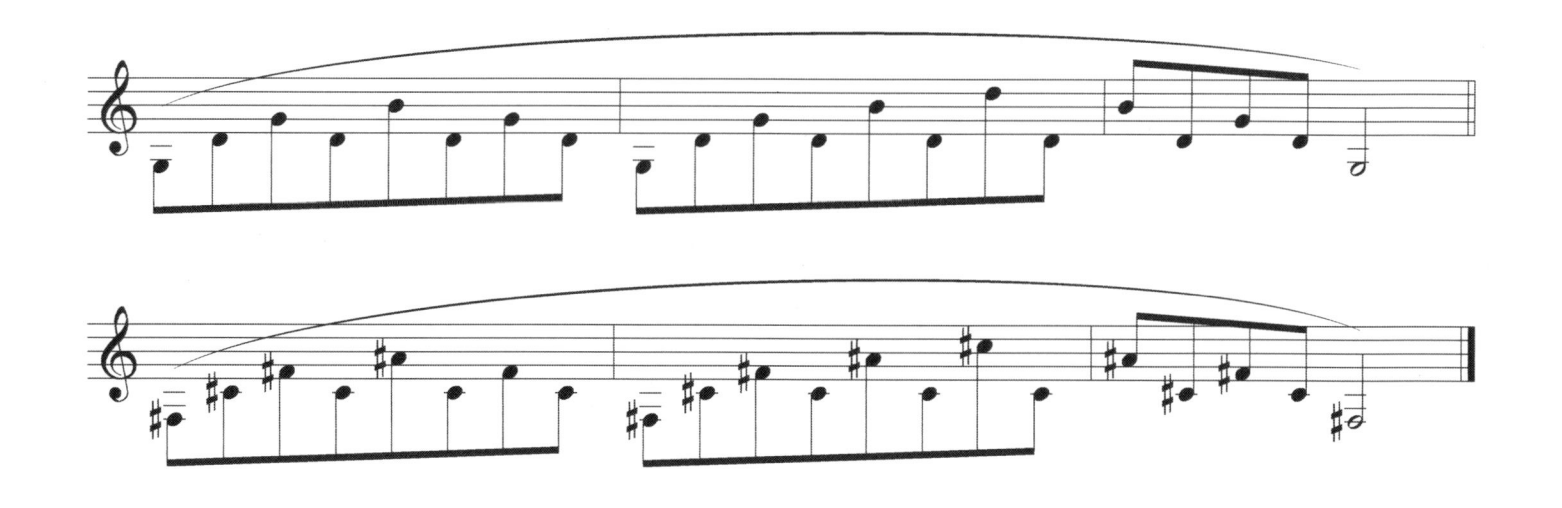

IV.

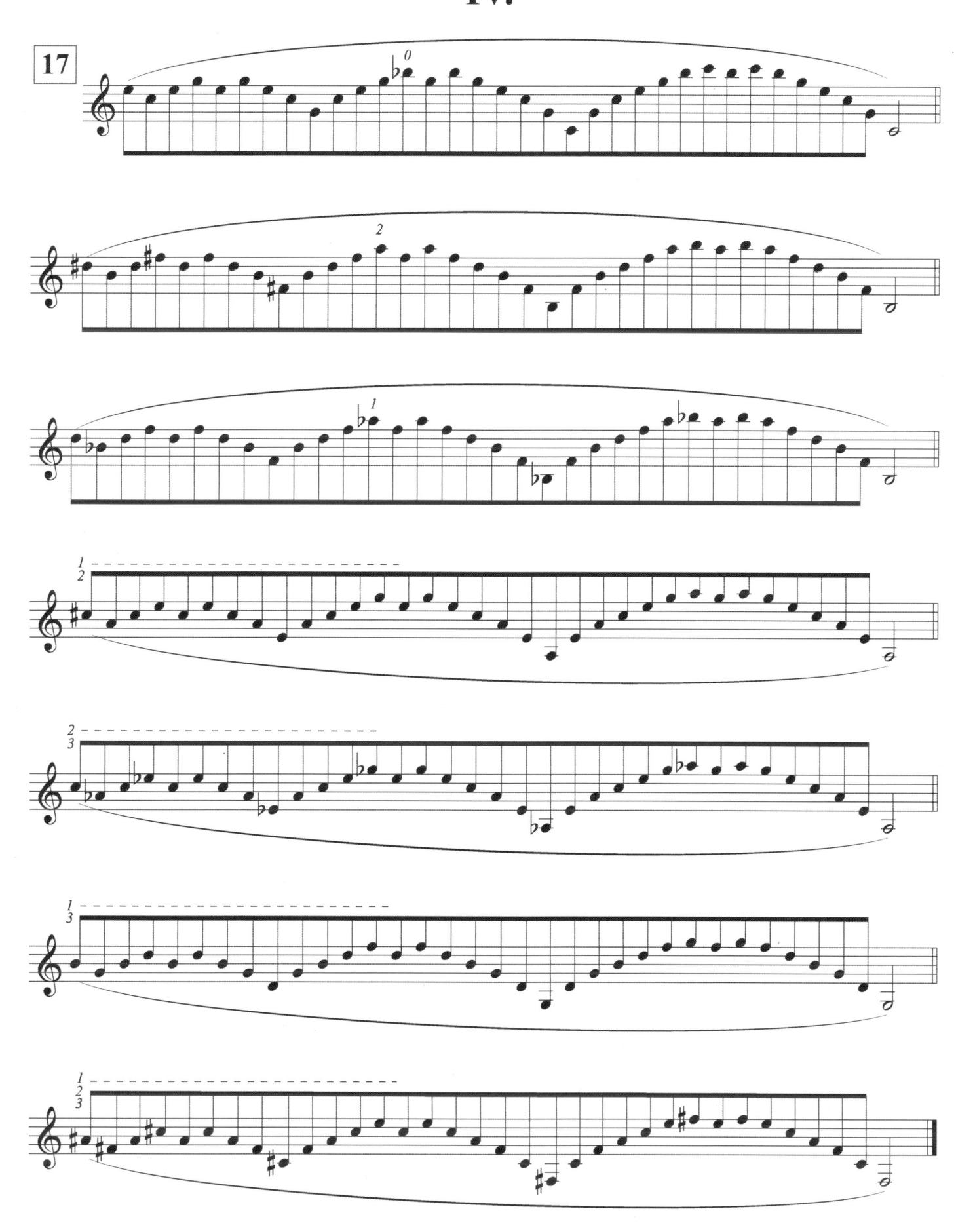

18

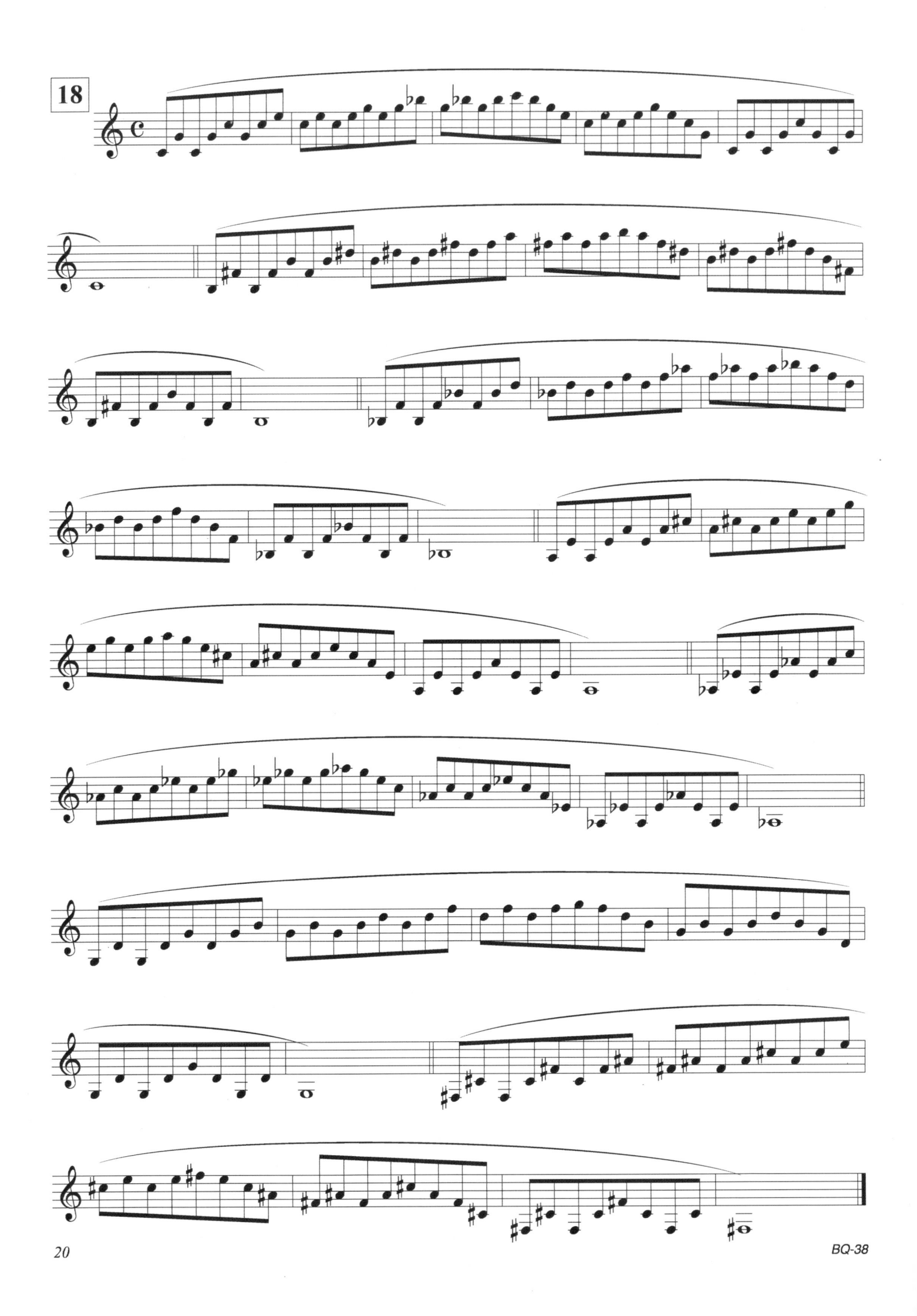

19

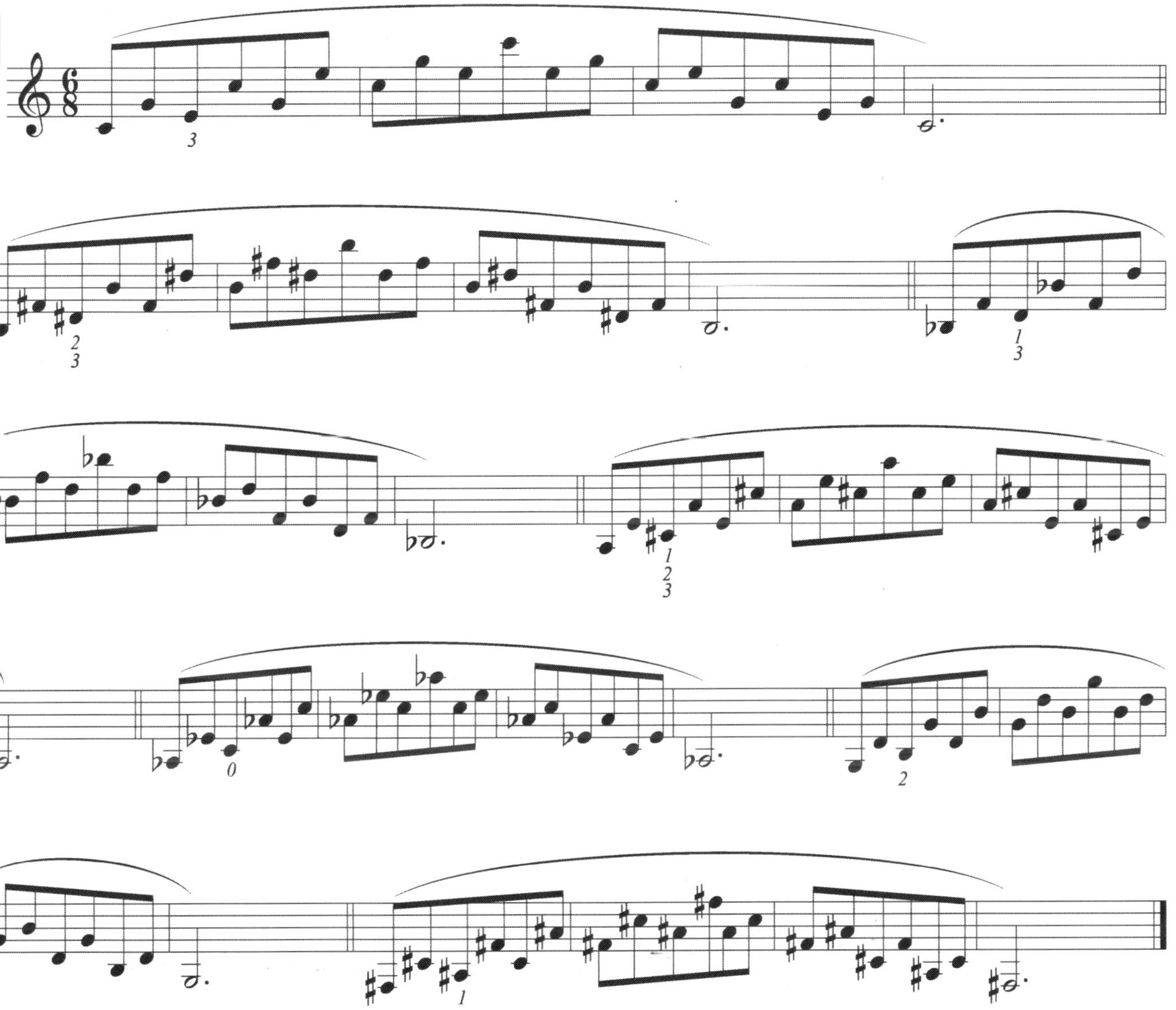

20

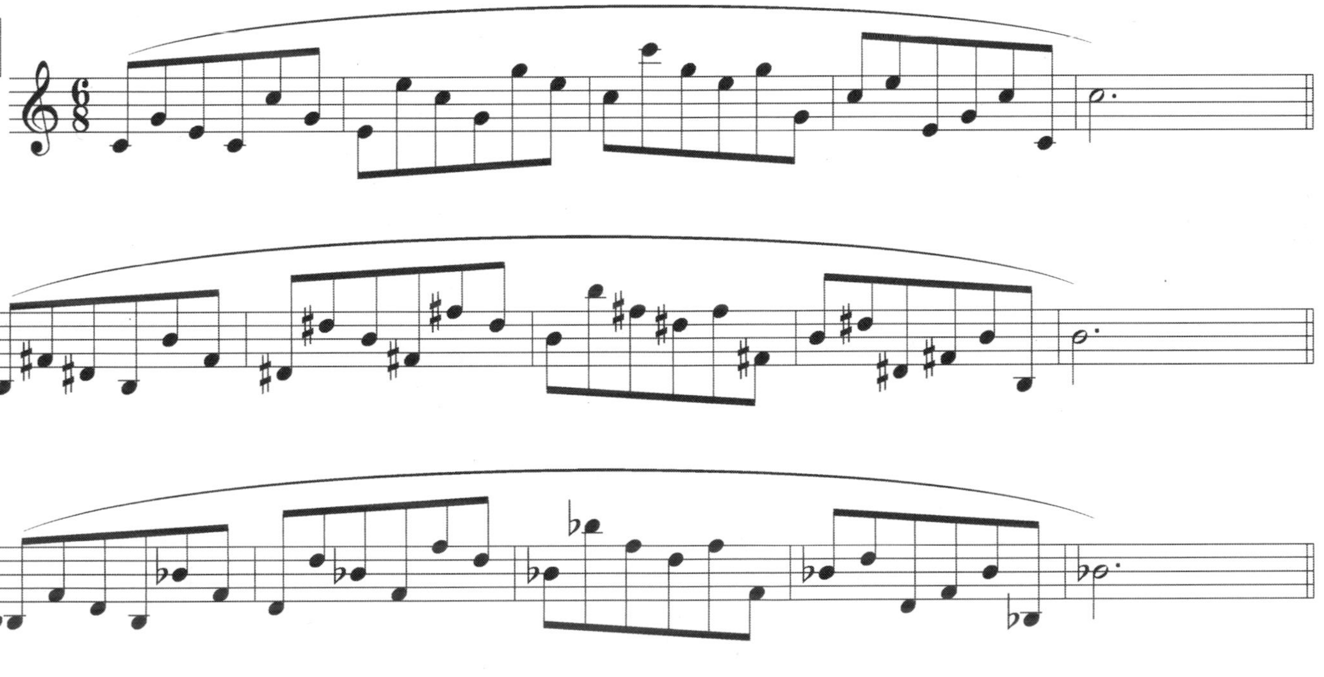

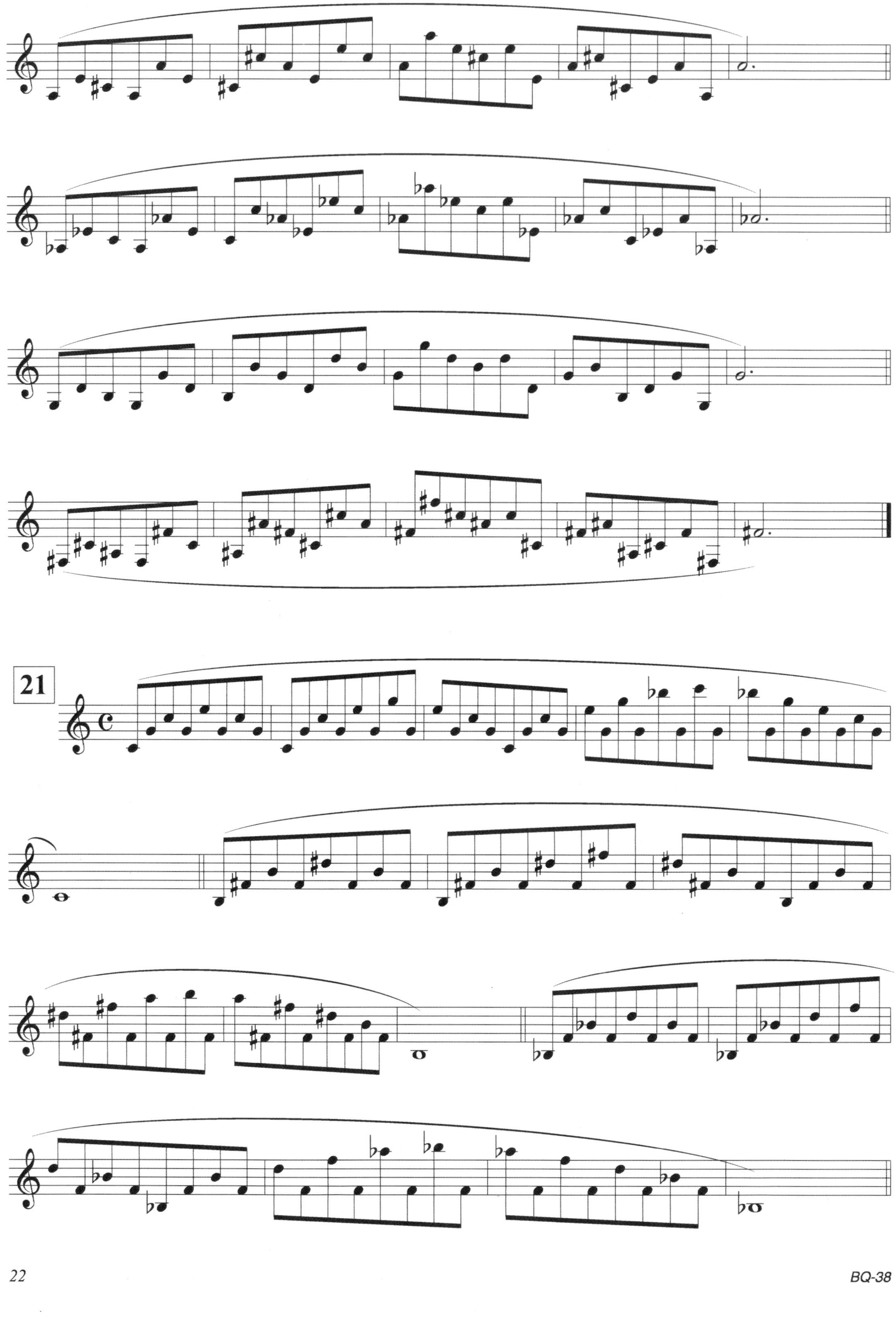
21

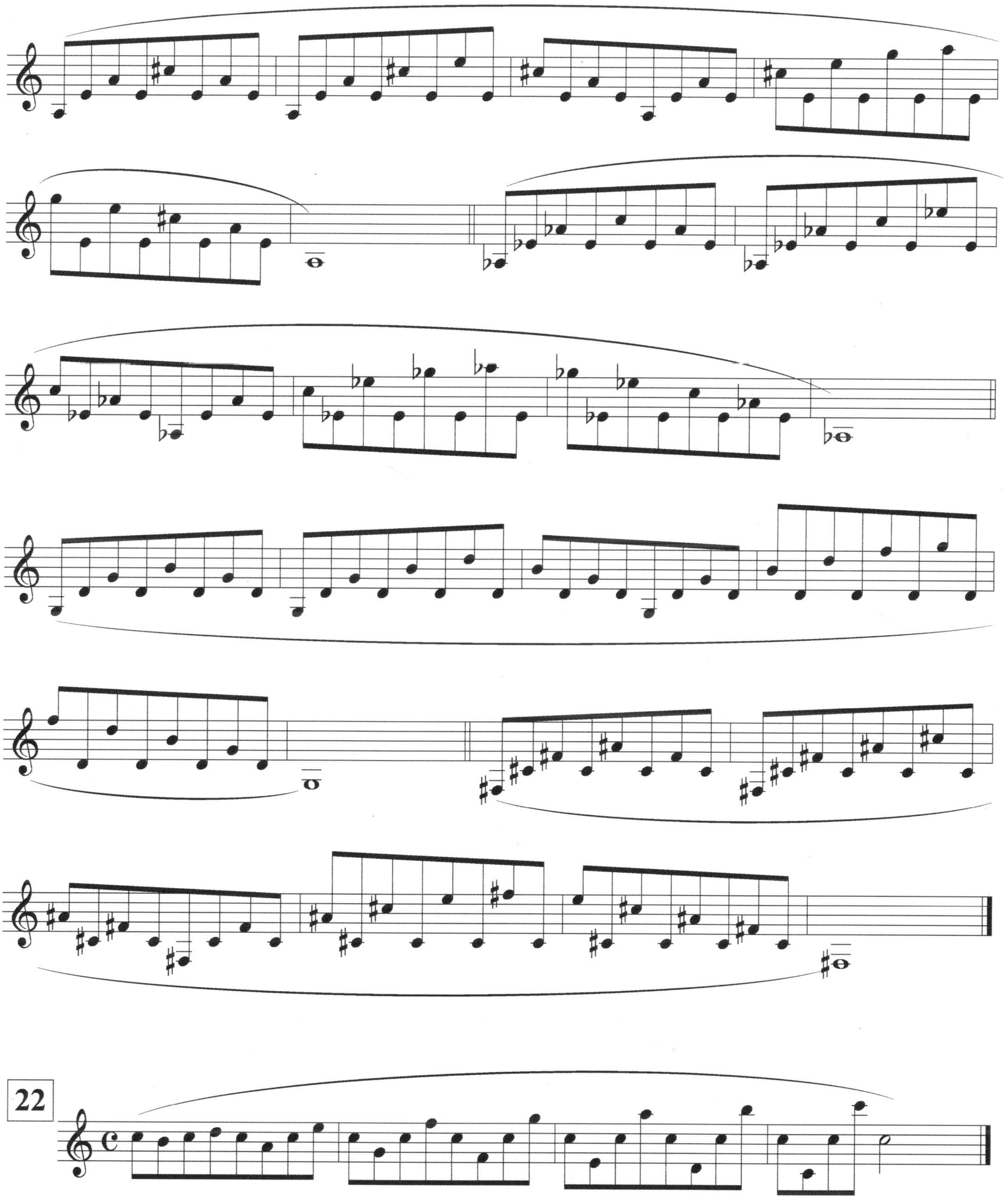
22

V.

25

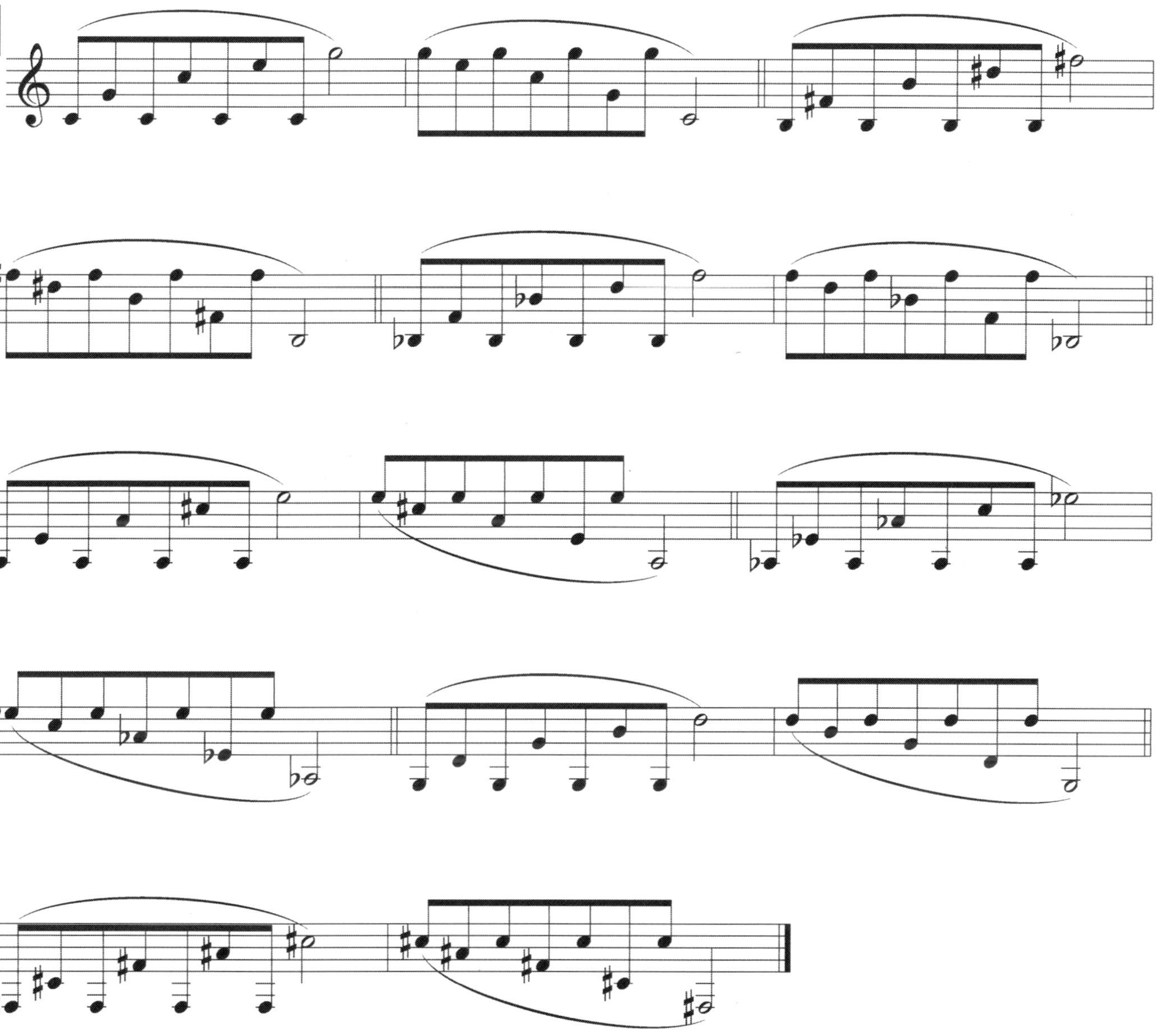

26

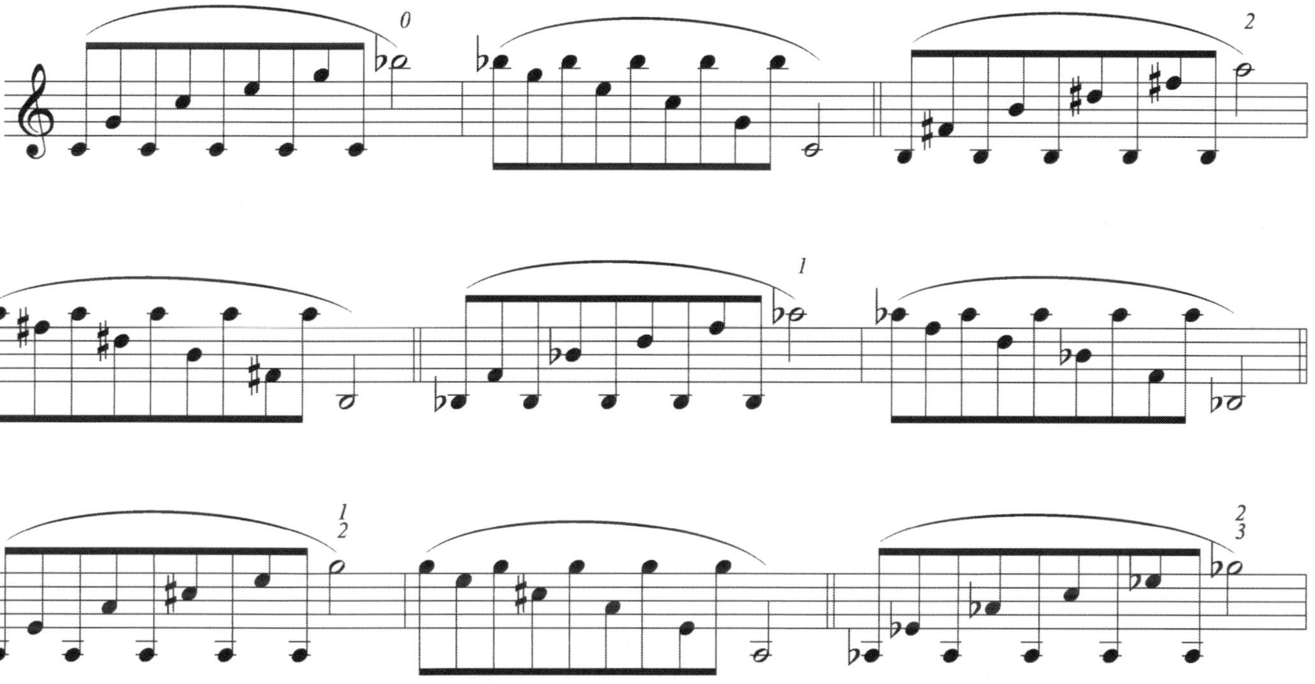

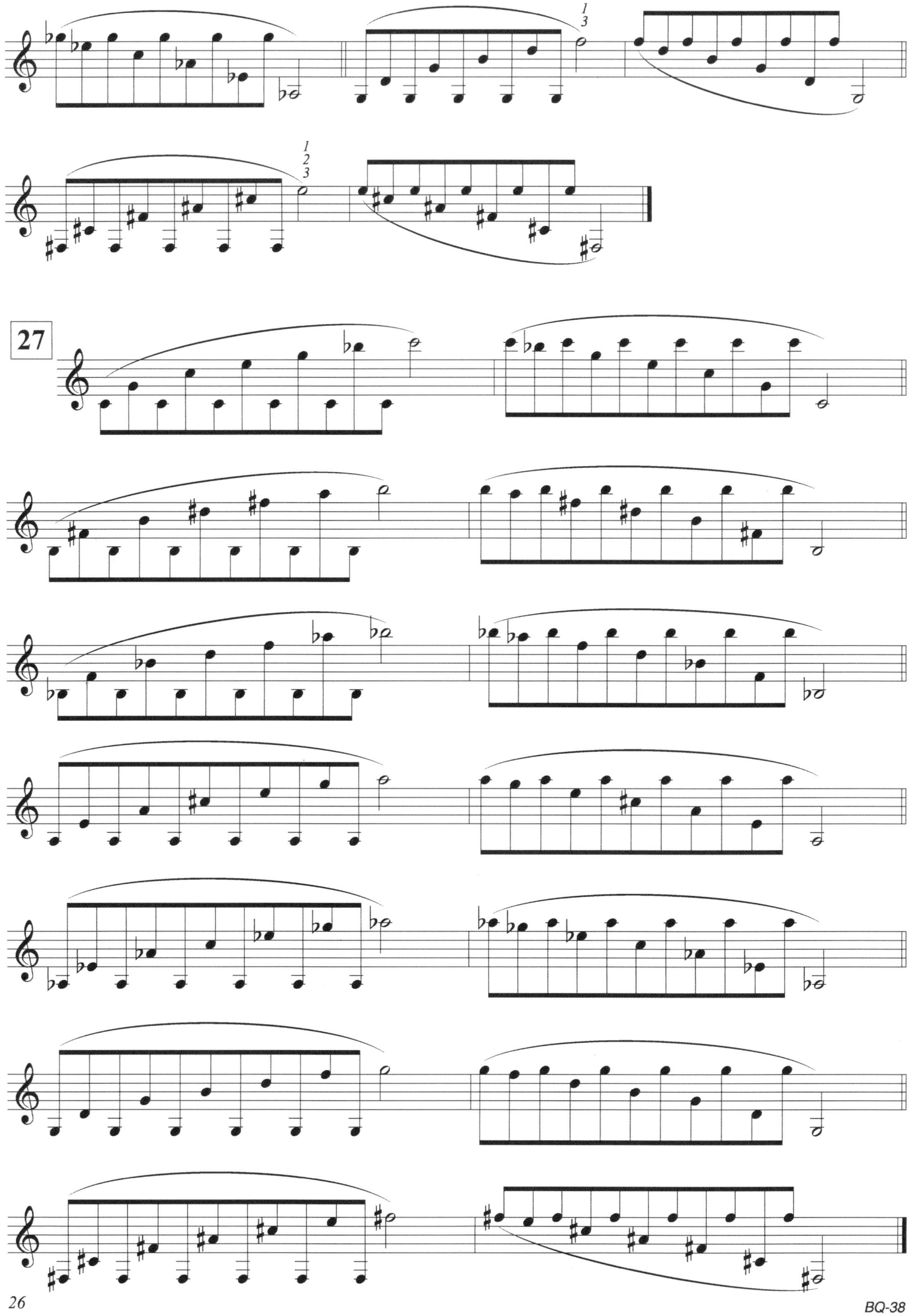
1
3
1
2
3
27

28

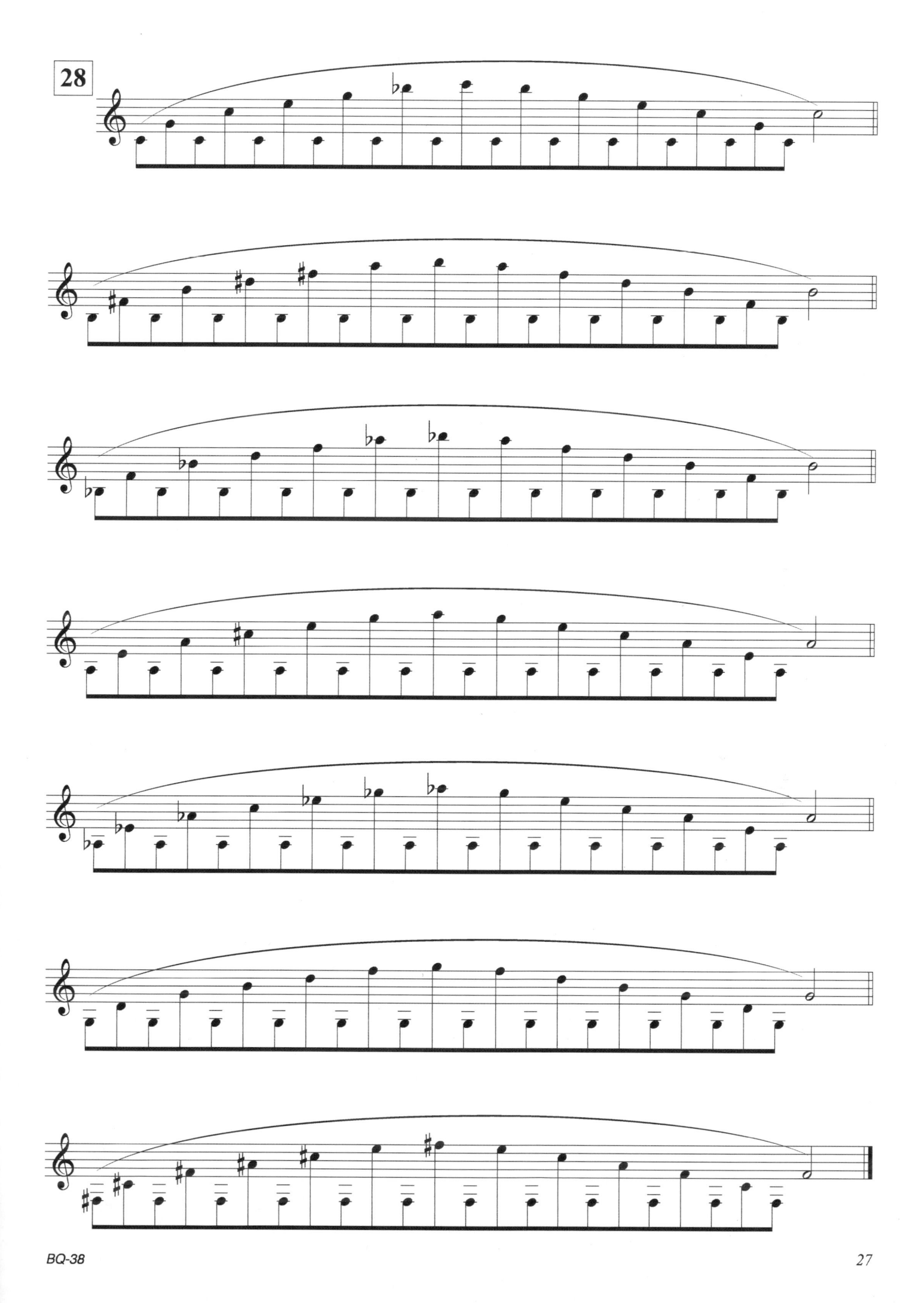

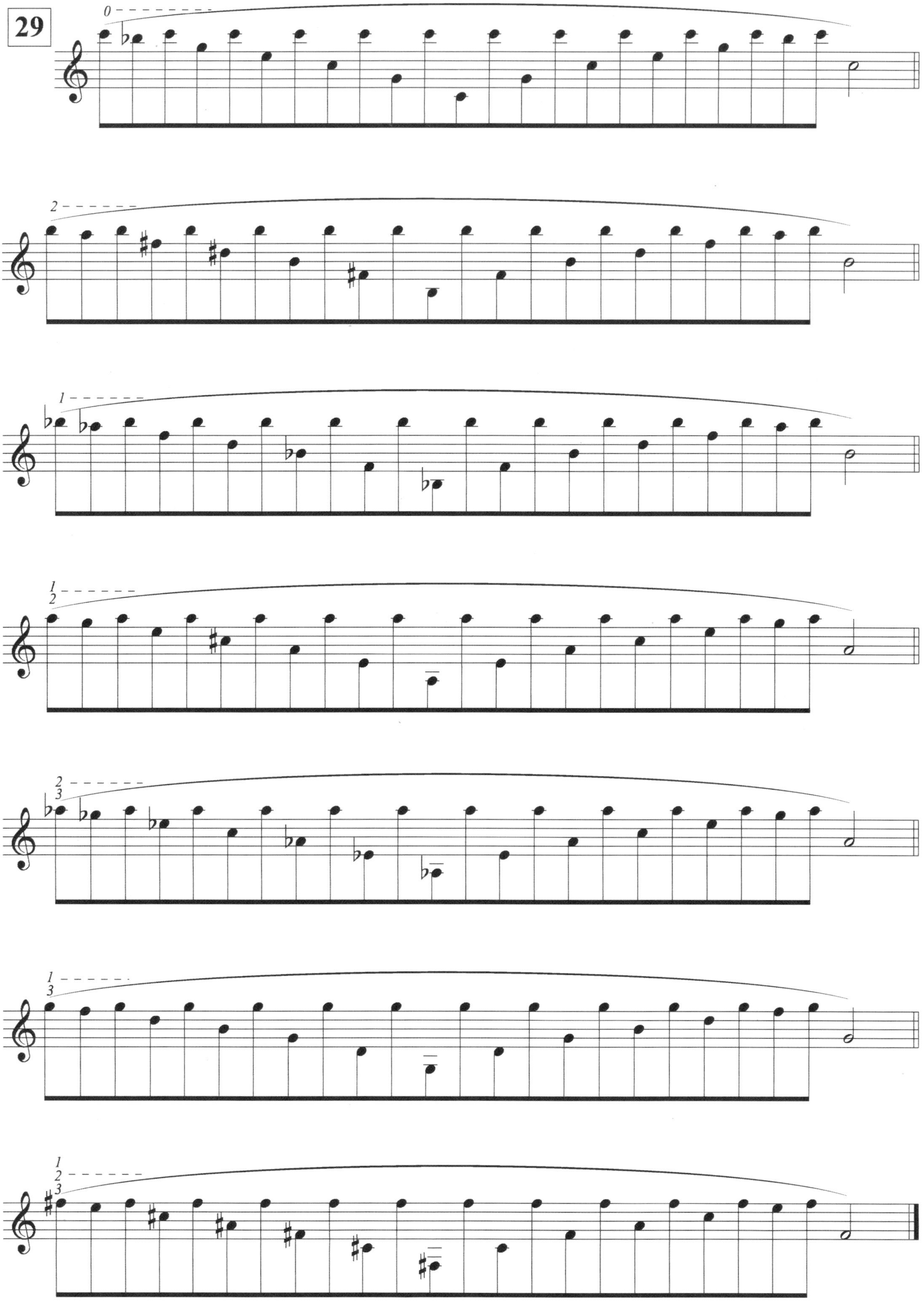
29

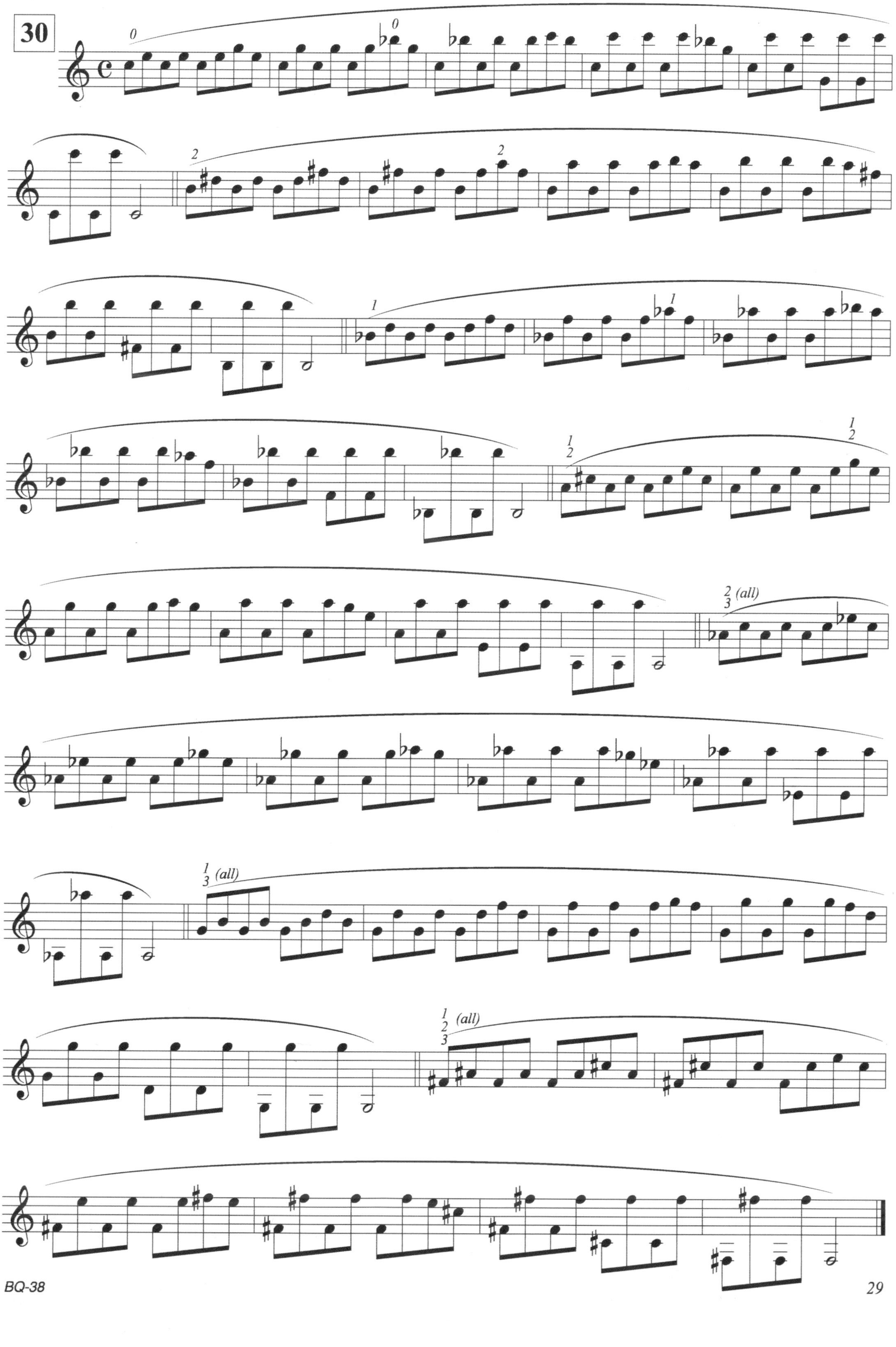
30
2 (all)
3
1
3 (all)
1
2 (all)
3

VI.

BQ-38

32

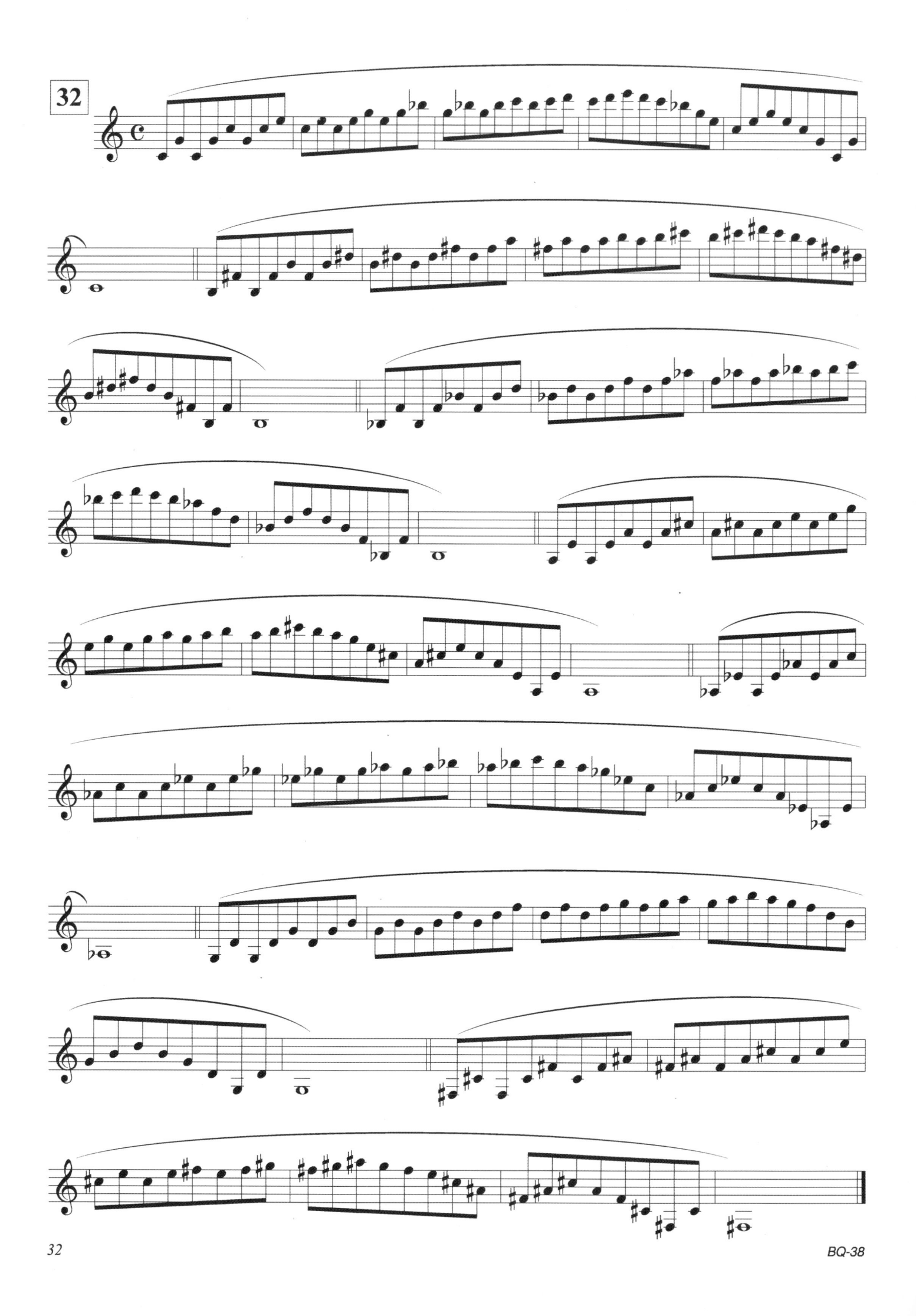

33

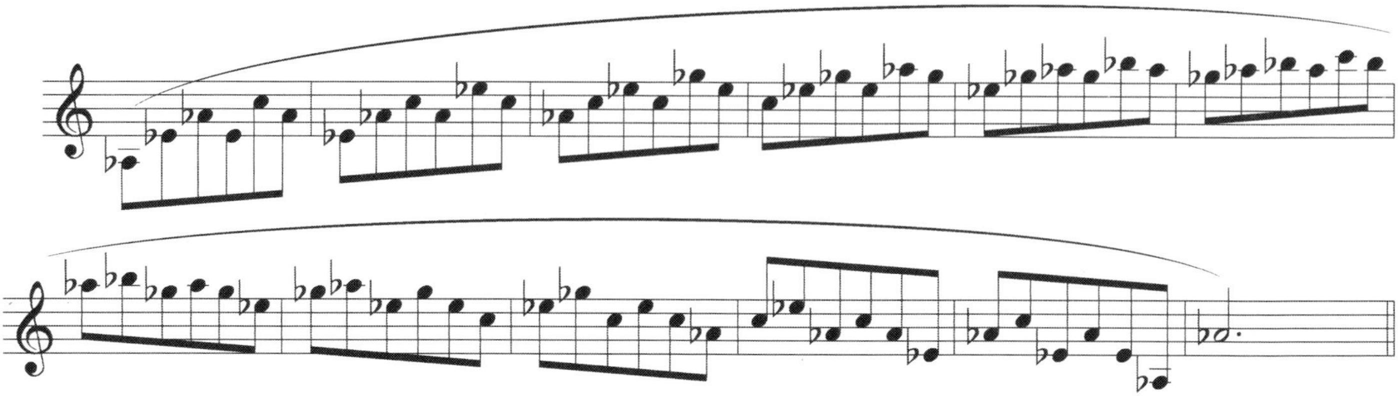

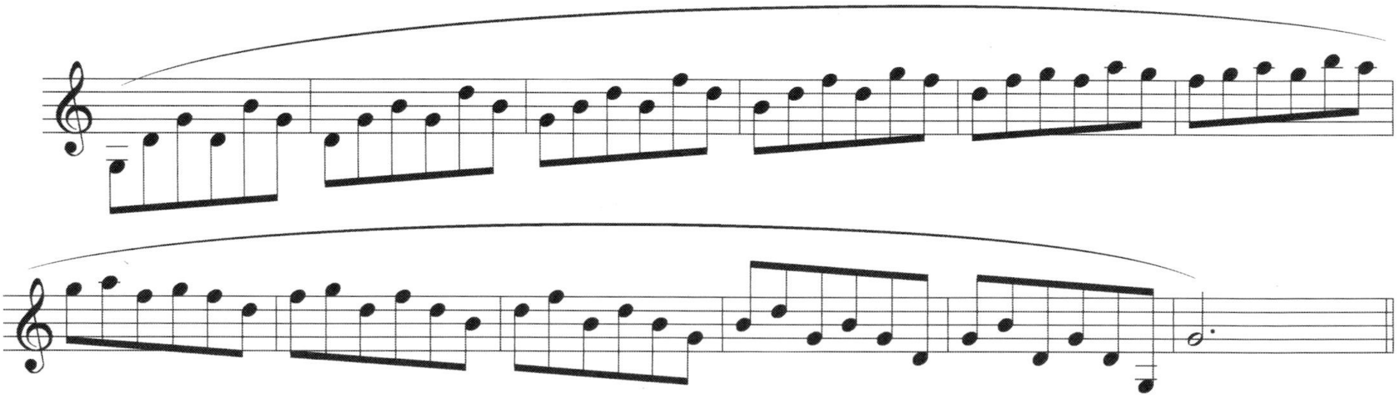

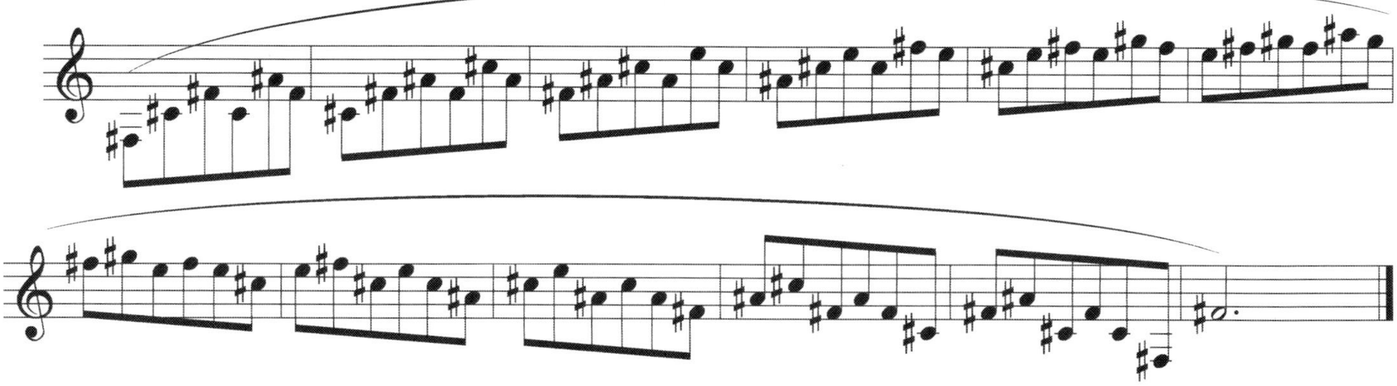

34

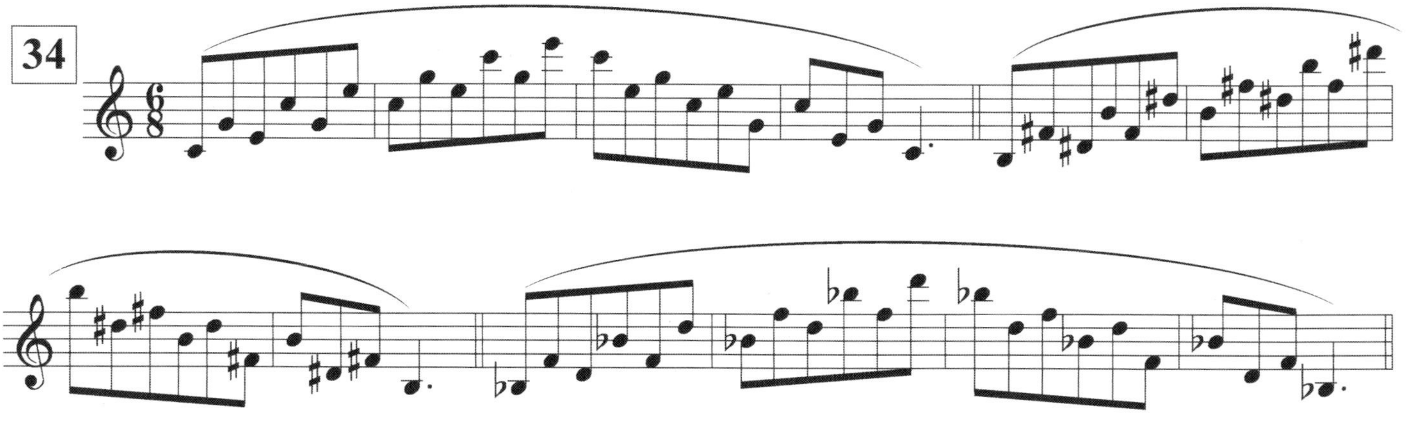

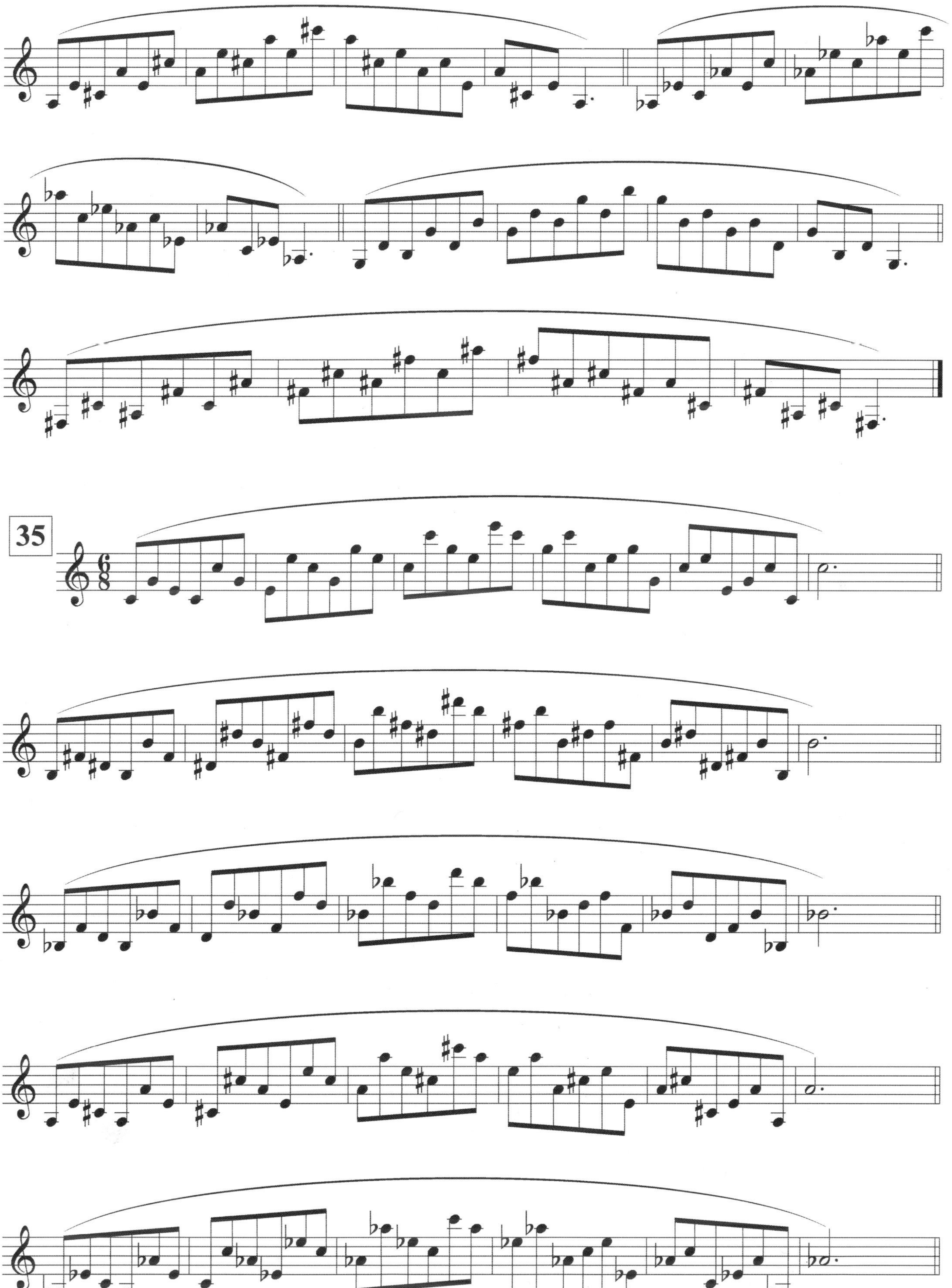
35

36

37

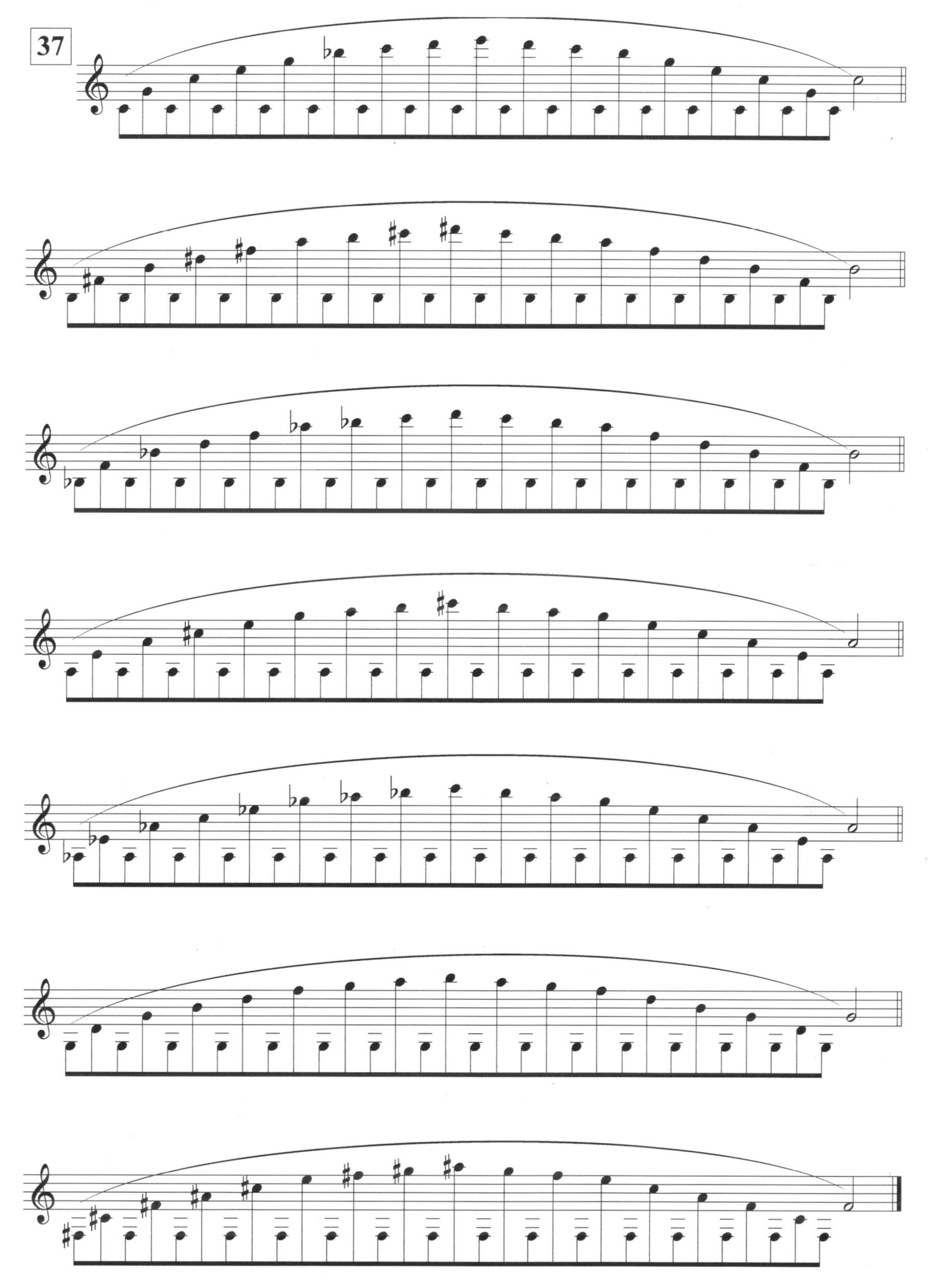

38

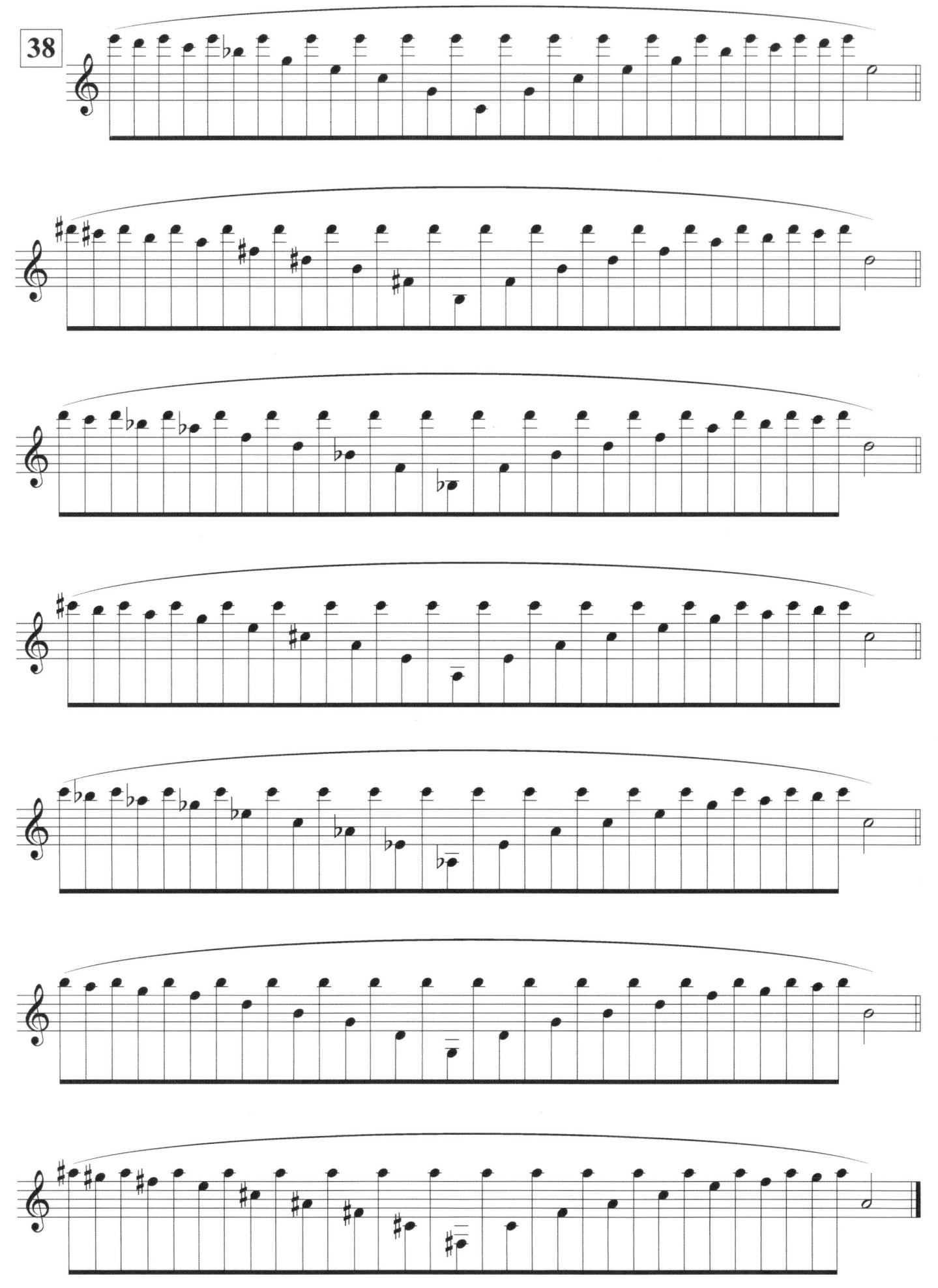

VII.

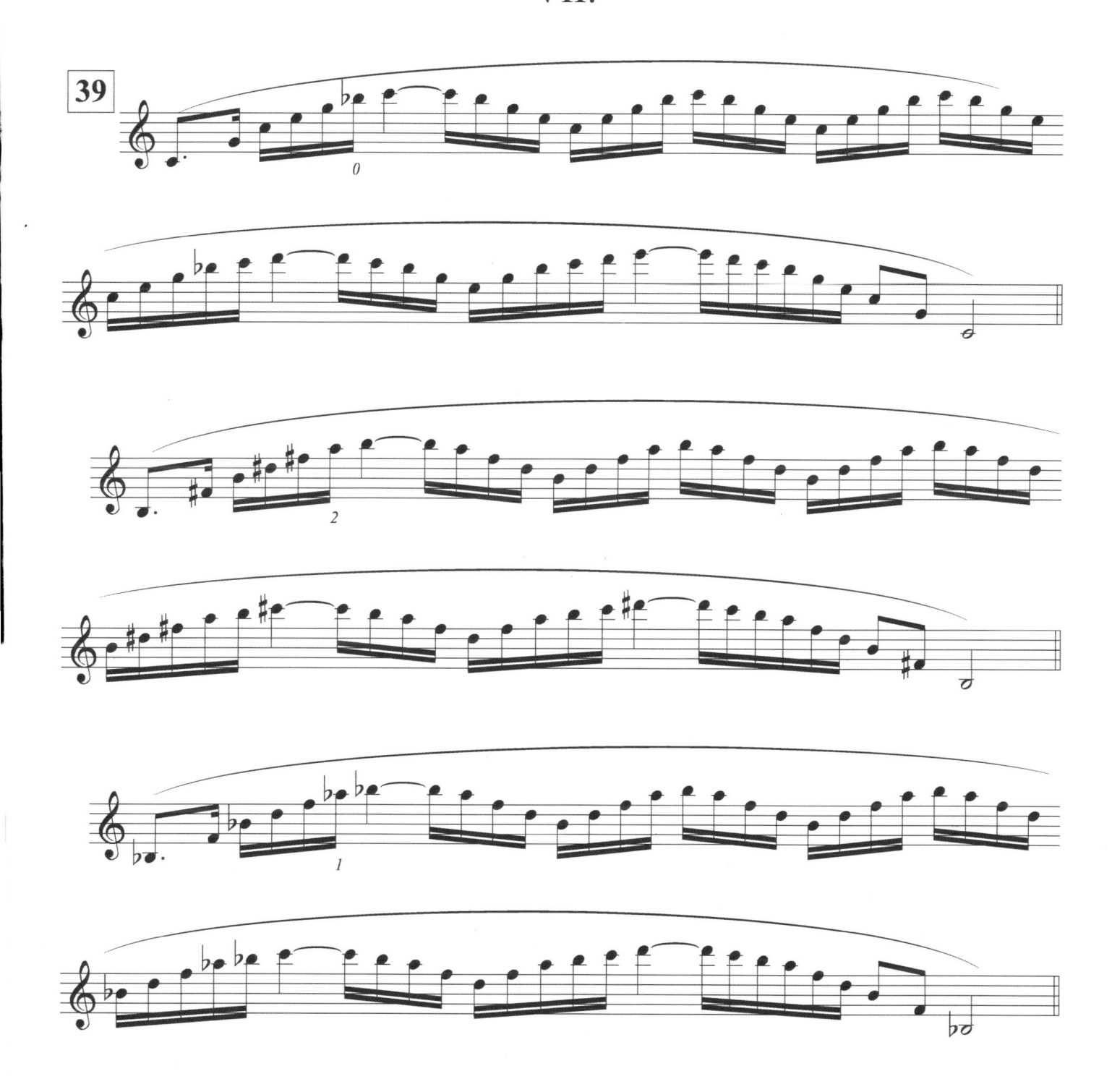

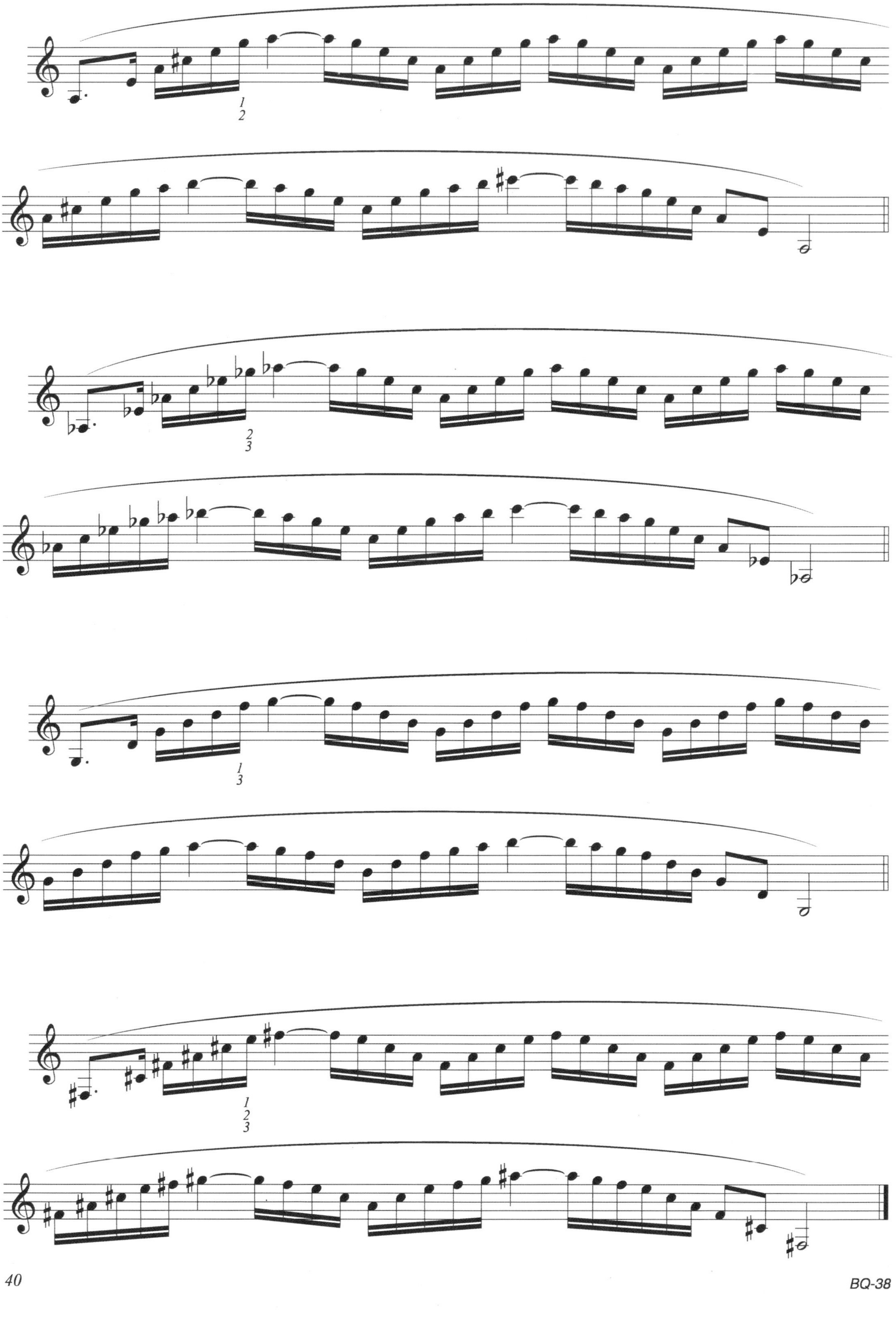
1
2
2
3
1
3
1
2
3